The $50 Home MAKEOVER

75 Easy Projects to Transform Your Current Space
Into Your Dream Place—for $50 or Less!

Shaunna West

Creator of *perfectly* imperfect

Foreword by Marian Parsons, author of *Inspired You*

A adams media

Avon, Massachusetts

Published by
Adams Media, a division of F+W Media, Inc.
57 Littlefield Street, Avon, MA 02322. U.S.A.
www.adamsmedia.com

ISBN 10: 1-4405-7117-1
ISBN 13: 978-1-4405-7117-6
eISBN 10: 1-4405-7118-X
eISBN 13: 978-1-4405-7118-3

Printed in the United States of America.

10   9   8   7   6   5   4   3   2   1

Library of Congress Cataloging-in-Publication Data
West, Shaunna.
  The $50 home makeover / Shaunna West, creator of perfectly imperfect.
      pages cm
  Includes index.
  ISBN 978-1-4405-7117-6 (pob) – ISBN 1-4405-7117-1 (pob) – ISBN 978-1-4405-7118-3 (ebook) – ISBN 1-4405-7118-X
(ebook)
  1. Interior decoration—Amateurs' manuals. I. Title. II. Title: Fifty dollar home makeover.
  NK2115.W46 2014
  747–dc23
                    2014008242

The following projects are the property and are under the copyright of the contributing bloggers and are used with permission: Gold Leaf and Faux Marble Coffee Table © Kristin Hunter, Chalkboard Wooden Placemats © Edie Wadsworth, Pleated Paper Wreath © Emily Jones, Reclaimed Wood Fence Art © Karianne Wood, Starched Fabric Feature Wall © Marian Parsons, Simple Map Wallpaper © Melissa Michaels, Fabric Frame Keepsake © Ashley Mills.

Cover design by Elisabeth Lariviere.
All other photos © Shaunna West.

This book is available at quantity discounts for bulk purchases.
For information, please call 1-800-289-0963.

Dedication

To my parents and my brother for believing in me, putting up with my childhood poetry, and for making me who I am . . .

My husband for supporting and loving me in the way only an amazing man could . . .

And to my children, Grayson and Ava, who inspire me every day.

Contents

CHAPTER 1

Before and After 27

Foreword

The world is full of decorating books. Ones that are filled with beautiful rooms decorated by high-end designers on outrageous budgets. Books that make you feel like your home, and maybe by extension you, will never measure up. Books that make decorating seem like a mysterious thing that you need a degree and a few initials after your name to do properly. Books that transform a rational woman into a crazy lady who isn't fun to live with because she's trying to make her home look like a magazine shoot 24/7. This is not one of those books.

My dear, talented friend, Shaunna, has written a decorating book for *you*. A real person, on a real budget, living in a real house. This is a book for the mom who craves a creative outlet, but only has five minutes to complete a project to satisfy that craving. This is a book for the newlyweds who want to make a bunch of hand-me-downs and thrift store finds look a little less like a bunch of hand-me-downs and thrift store finds. This is a book for the people who want a wow-factor kind of home without breaking the bank.

But even more than that—more than the creative ideas, fun projects, expert painting tips, and inspirational pictures—Shaunna gives you permission to try and fail. She encourages you to put things into perspective. And you'll close this book at the end, feeling that you've just made a new friend. The kind of friend who dishes her best secrets and tricks with you. One who gives you the push to try something new and cheers you on. One who's willing to share her perfectly imperfect life and home with you. That's the kind of decorating book you're about to read. And you're in for a real treat.

—**MARIAN PARSONS**, author of *Inspired You*, creator of Miss Mustard Seed's Milk Paint, and blogger at *Miss Mustard Seed*

Preface

Writing this book is surreal for me. It shouldn't be; I go through the same writing rituals almost daily for my blog. But I've dreamed of writing a book since I was a little girl, thinking up stories of mermaids, lagoons, and adventure. If you had told me that one day I'd write a blog for hundreds of thousands of readers about life, design, DIY projects, and the general imperfection of it all, I would have laughed you out of the room.

I was a late-blooming DIYer. The crafting, painting, and decorating came later for me. After college, I married the goofy love of my life and promptly decorated our new home the way everyone else decorated—think commercial/matchy-matchy/brown furniture. There's nothing *wrong* with brown, but there is something wrong with surrounding yourself with a space that's not wholly you.

A few years later, after having my second child, I found myself craving more life, more inspiration, more everything for the little family I so cherished. On Christmas Day in 2009, I sat surrounded by crumpled wrapping paper and love all around. The need to write was so overwhelming I could taste it, and with that, the blog *Perfectly Imperfect* was born.

I really thought I was writing for me (and maybe for my mom and dad), but you know what? People started reading . . . real, live humans that were not related to me. It was thrilling, humbling, mind-blowing.

My husband, Matt (who you'll see a lot of in this book), and I were in the middle of an attic renovation, and we were going with our gut in the decorating department, even though we had no formal training in architecture or design. We created our writing room, playroom, and home theater, and they were completely us. Creating those rooms on a budget led to an entire home transformation.

These makeovers are what got our blog moving around the World Wide Web, and they've been featured by (pinch me!) *The Nate Berkus Show, Better Homes & Gardens, Cottages & Bungalows, Flea Market Style, Design Sponge, The Pioneer Woman, Apartment Therapy's Color Contest,* Pottery Barn, Pottery Barn Kids, and Tori Spelling's *EdiTORIal,* to name a few.

Somewhere in the middle of all that hoopla, it hit me: You can have the home you want . . . *now.* It may be a work in progress, but you can create spaces that are completely you and that inspire you every moment of every day. Our homes matter. Our families share everything there, and those moments become our lives. So where we share them—it matters.

Perfectly Imperfect then became a mission for us to empower you to pick up a paintbrush or a nail gun to create the home you want now. To go for it, and celebrate life's imperfections. and create amid them anyway. *You* are what this is all about. Your homes, your lives, your families, and the imperfect beauty that lies within them all.

Because we fell in love with inspiring our readers to create their own havens, we opened a retail shop, Perfectly Imperfect (no surprise on the name), in our hometown square in Troy, Alabama. Soon after, we made our decor available in our online shop (*www.perfectlyimperfectshop.com*) and the rest, as they say, is history.

It has been some time since we opened our shop, and to say that we have been blessed is the understatement of the century. We continue to meet readers and customers, one after another, and with each encounter the drive to keep doing what we love grows.

There are big things on the horizon at *Perfectly Imperfect*, including the publication of this book, and we are so excited to see where it all leads. So come along with us for this part of the journey . . . it's going to be a good one.

Introduction

Do you love every room in your home? Or do you have rooms that seem dark and outdated, or furniture that doesn't reflect your style anymore? Do you dream of creating a home that feels exactly like you, but don't have the budget, the time, or even a clue where to start? This book will help you stop dreaming, and start doing.

Here you'll find 75 of the very easiest, most affordable, most high-impact projects—all of which can be completed with $50 or less. These simple projects will help you squeeze every last drop of style out of every cent, so that you get big improvements, but not a big bill.

This isn't a book about how to style your grand piano or pick out granite for your butler's pantry. It's a book for the real world, where you're stuck with a hideous chartreuse wall your landlord won't let you paint over, or you've spent your last penny on a home to call your own . . . but that straight-out-of-'80s kitchen is now also yours. It's about working with what you have to make your dream home a reality today.

If you're anything like me, you don't have the time or energy to hand-make every piece of decor for your home. These are the projects that are really worth the time and expense, so that you can create the home of your dreams without putting your life on hold. You won't find weekend warrior demolitions or magazine-worthy room makeovers here, but you'll be inspired to tackle easy tasks that can instantly infuse personality into your home.

This guide is filled with affordable, quick afternoon projects—everything from semi-handmade wreaths to painted furniture makeovers to simple builds, like our Pallet Wall Clock. Hate your outdated builder-grade cabinets? Turn to the Painted Builder-Grade Cabinets project in Chapter 1, and you'll find an easy $30 makeover to make them look brand new and beautiful again. If you're coveting an expensive, dramatic chandelier, you'll find a simple Lantern Chandelier tutorial in Chapter 4 for creating your own stunning light fixture—for just $10! Or if you're stuck with a laminate countertop you don't love but can't afford to replace, try the two-hour, high-impact Painted Laminate Countertops project in Chapter 1. Have half an hour to spare? Create beautiful, magazine-worthy Gold Leaf Botanical Prints to brighten your walls with the step-by-step instructions in Chapter 3.

You'll also find beautiful photographs of every single project, and many with step-by-step photographs. Each project is simply labeled with icons for cost, difficulty, and time, and the project sidebars are full of extra tips and inspiration. Sprinkled throughout are several amazing projects from other top home design bloggers—we could not be more excited about sharing their creativity with you.

This is a tool for the everyday homeowner, and the everyday home. Get ready to be inspired to pick up a paintbrush, tackle that intimidating space, and to create the home you want, one project at a time. Let's get started!

How to Use This Book

If I could give you one tip about how to use this book, it would be this: Forget the rules and have fun; this is about *your* time, *your* family, *your* home. These projects range from ten-minute drawer fronts to an afternoon of building a simple end table. Creating the home you want is a process. You don't need a fancy degree, and you certainly don't have to hire a professional to do it for you. One of the most freeing things I ever did was grasp that my home was mine to make my own. This book is your guide to just that: freeing yourself so that you can make your home your own.

Taking the reins to paint, swap out a throw pillow, or build a coffee table isn't a life-altering decision. But it *can* be life altering when you feel like your home works for you and reflects your style. At the end of the day, this book is about putting your feet up in the home you crave on the budget you have.

ON STARTING SMALL

I didn't grow up painting and drawing and sewing. I didn't decorate my own room, and I certainly didn't go diving through junk stores to dig up treasure. The idea of creating my own anything was pretty foreign to me, so when my husband suggested we paint my childhood furniture instead of buying new pieces for our upcoming bundle of joy, I all but laughed him out of the room. I literally remember thinking, "Why would we ruin this nice furniture?!"

I was six months pregnant, and painting that first nightstand on our back porch was absolutely terrifying to me. But I liked the way the brush felt in my hand, and I liked the fact that I was working on something— that I had a project. I liked that at the end of the day, my son's nightstand was snow white instead of yellowed-cream. And it had cost me about two hours and twenty bucks.

What do you need? What does your home lack? Start with the projects you are most excited about and the ones you feel your home is begging for. Start small. Start somewhere. Just start.

ON REMEMBERING TO LIVE

Once you begin painting, scraping, and decorating toward a whole new home, you will become addicted. I'm telling you . . . once that first room is finished, and you look at it and smile each time you pass it by, you will be an addicted DIYer.

Here's the thing, though: The adrenaline will wear off eventually, and even if it doesn't, remember why you are painting/crafting/sewing/building. You are doing all these projects to create a simpler life, to make your home work for you.

Be sure that throughout the process you take time to rest, and time to simply live. I'm telling myself this, too; we are notorious for starting six major projects at once. The process is thrilling for the first two weeks, and somewhere around week three, there are mounds of dust, toys everywhere, and we can't even find our kitchen sink.

As you catch the DIY bug, pace yourself. Try to finish projects you begin, try to stick to one room makeover at a time, and hey, take a break when you need it.

ON WORKING WITH YOUR MOTIVATION

Unless you are going to begin your own decorating blog, or construction company, or interior design firm, this work on your home is going to happen in your leisure time and should be enjoyable. Some weekends you'll feel like tackling the world, or at least building a new entertainment center, and some weekends you'll be thankful you felt like dusting.

Go with it; work with your own motivation. You'll find that you get triple the amount done if you work while motivated instead of making yourself paint a room every weekend off. Using this approach to fixing up your home really helps you avoid burnout. Oh, and it can also aid you in keeping your kitchen sink visible and free of stacks of dishes.

ON THE NOTION OF PERFECTION

Just like painting my son's nightstand was terrifying to me, it might be terrifying to you to start one of these projects you'd desperately like to try.

Do yourself a favor: Decide that some won't work. It'll be humid while you're hot-gluing to your heart's content, and the stuff just won't set. You might paint with two colors I love in my home, but in your south-facing room, they might look yellow instead of white. Despite admiring a photo of our mirrored chest, you may paint your own and decide the piece is just too shiny for your taste.

Creating—it's a process. It is not, however, a process of perfection. It took me three times to get the correct wash of color I wanted for the Dyed Fabric Napkins in Chapter 2. There will be projects that you complete and love, and others that just don't work in your home or need a little tweaking. I'm betting that you'll love all these projects, but never be afraid to tweak them so that they're a reflection of you. If you don't like a paint color, swap it. If the furniture is too shiny, put some dark wax on it. Repaint it, even. No creation is perfect, but no project is ever complete until you, and only you, are happy with it.

ON PINTEREST AND BLOGS

It wouldn't hurt more blogs or Pinterest gurus to share their worst rooms and their "failures" with the world. It is quite easy for you to peruse Pinterest for ten minutes and leave feeling inadequate, frustrated, and kind of annoyed.

When you look at a decorating blog (even mine), remember that the room reveal was shot with beautiful lighting, staged accessories, and clutter-free moments. That's why we like to share some pretty embarrassing photographs with you from time to time on our blog. We're all about keeping it real.

Your project, space, or furniture may get dirty or chipped by day-to-day life, but so does everyone else's. Remember that a snapshot of a project is just that—a fleeting moment.

Plus, all those mistakes and chips and dents make for a life lived with character, right?

ON THE PROJECTS

These 75 projects are broken down into four categories: Before and After, Semi-Handmade, Upcycling, and Simple DIY. Turn to the Before and After section for furniture makeovers, painting techniques, and simple updates. The Semi-Handmade section boasts crafting projects that call for premade materials to begin with, so you save time and effort. Think wreaths assembled from purchased elements, stenciled pillow covers, and easy chalkboard placemats. In the Upcycling section, you'll find new ways to use old objects or ways to reinvent items you already own. You'll love the Suitcases Side Table, Vintage Art Collection (such an affordable way to add personality and style to your walls!), and the Book Letters. The Simple DIY section shares beginner-level building projects and projects that require a few more steps, but are not necessarily more difficult. You will love the Simple Map Wallpaper, Starched Fabric Feature Wall, Wood Slat End Table, and Antique Door Table.

You'll also find a simple project key with icons that denote cost, difficulty, and time. Every one of these projects was completed for $50 or less, and many of them cost only a few dollars—some were even free! We listed an approximate cost, but remember that pricing in different locations varies, and sometimes we use the same can of paint for more than one project, lowering our cost. Different types of paint and fabric will cost more or less, so keep that in mind.

PROJECT KEY

Every project has a project key where you'll find three things: the cost, difficulty, and time needed for that project.

💰 COST

The cost of a project will indicate how much you'll spend to recreate it exactly as pictured. The estimate only includes the cost of what is actually used. For example, for the Painted Laminate Countertops in Chapter 1, I calculated only the cost for the amount of paint used, not the entire container of paint. If a project calls for repurposing a piece of furniture, then the original cost of the furniture wasn't included in the calculation. Many of the projects use the same tools, such as paintbrushes or sanding blocks, so those weren't calculated as a new expense for every project. I tried to round up in my calculations to give you a true picture of cost, but of course, you could reduce the cost by choosing cheaper brands and reusing what you have already. Also keep in mind that product cost may vary from place to place.

🖌 DIFFICULTY

The level of difficulty of each project is indicated by stars in the project key. For example, a one-star project is easier than a project with four stars.

★–★: This project is easy-peasy. It requires few tools and little effort.

★★: This project is a bit more difficult, requiring more attention to detail or instruction, but it's still simple to create.

★★★–★★★★: These projects are more difficult. They will require some more intensive work, such as cutting or nailing or even using layers of paint to create a finish. However, if instructions are followed, no project should be too difficult!

🕐 TIME

I recorded exactly how much time each project took me. Most of these projects were done in an unplanned way, meaning I did not have materials lying out in a perfect assembly line (of course not!), so the timelines should be close to what you can realistically pull off yourself. Everyone works differently, though, and you may take breaks when I didn't or have unexpected events to deal with. Just keep working, and the project will get finished!

TOOL KIT

This book is all about really affordable, easy projects. Most projects have similar supply lists, so you won't need to buy a bunch of new supplies that you may only use once. All projects were created with simplicity in mind. You can also use the heck out of each can of paint—one quart of paint can be used on six or seven different projects.

While you will have a supply list for each project, we thought it would be helpful to list our favorites here in the Tool Kit, along with a short explanation as to why we love them.

I will also tell you when we believe certain products are best for certain projects. We choose our products very carefully, and we've always loved the way our projects turn out with certain brands. But feel free to substitute more inexpensive products to save money. And don't run out and buy everything here—this is just a handy reference if you'd like to read more about why certain products work well.

Annie Sloan Chalk Paint, Miss Mustard Seed's Milk Paint, Acrylic Paint, and Soft Waxes

You'll find these three paints throughout the book, used on everything from furniture to lamps to glass to scrap boards. These paints contain very low (or no) VOCs. VOCs stand for volatile organic compounds. The EPA regulates how many VOCs are emitted to prevent too many chemicals and toxins from polluting our air. Low (or no) VOCs is the way to go! These paints flow off the brush nicely—there are virtually no brushstrokes in the finish—and they create timeworn looks so effortlessly.

I recommend using Annie Sloan Soft Wax or Miss Mustard Seed's Furniture Wax as a topcoat and sealant. They both create a smooth, lustrous finish that is easily doctored when nicked or scratched. It's no secret that Marian of Miss Mustard Seed is a dear friend of mine, but I recommend her products because I absolutely love them and believe in them. As a matter of fact, her milk paint has been used all throughout our home!

Brushes

You can use all sorts of different brushes for painting and crafting. My favorites, though, are a Purdy 2½" sash nylon brush for smooth finishes or with Miss Mustard Seed's Milk Paint, and an Annie Sloan small brush for rustic finishes, crafts, and artistry. I also love the Martha Stewart craft brushes, as well as those from IKEA.

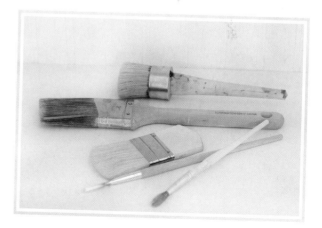

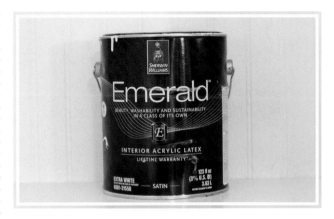

Favorite Latex Paint

Latex paint still has my heart for some projects. I love Sherwin Williams paint, and am especially fond of their new Emerald line, as well as the ProClassic line for whites. Both of these are durable, dry to a hard finish, and require no topcoat. Use them for sprayed or rolled finishes on cabinets, painted floors, and bookcases. Tip: If you are painting furniture with latex paint and don't have access to a paint sprayer, paint in the grooves first with a Purdy brush, and then use a sponge roller to paint the flat surfaces. Latex paint samples are also great for small projects, so that you don't have to commit to a whole can of paint in a color you may never use again.

Chalkboard Paint

Almost every surface is better with chalkboard paint. It's truly a magical medium, transforming the dullest surfaces into chalkboards. Both the spray can and the quart size are great. The spray is best for small items, and a brush or roller is best for large flat surfaces.

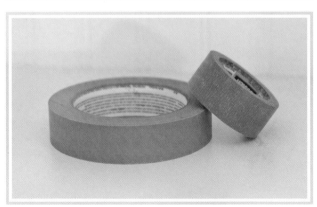

Painter's Tape

There are a few types of painter's tape, but I've found that FrogTape is the best. You'll never get any paint seeping under the tape, or have peeling when removing the tape. It works well on many surfaces, even fabric (see our Striped Curtains in Chapter 1).

Washi and Decorative Tape

I have a thing for washi tape and other pretty tapes. It adds just the right touch to simple tags, gifts, and paper displays, and now there are lots of decorative tapes that tackle home projects as well (see the Duct Tape End Table and Washi Tape Drawer Fronts in Chapter 1). You can order colored duct tape from Amazon, and the thicker washi tapes I like are made by MT Casa (*www.mtcasa.com*).

X-ACTO Knife

This little guy is one of the best crafting tools to have around. You'll want it for several projects in the book (see Washi Tape Striped Steps, Duct Tape End Table, and Giftwrap-Backed Bookcase), and you may find that you'll start using it all the time at home. Snazzy, super-sharp cutting tool? Check.

Power Tools

There are a million handy power tools out there, but here are some favorites.

» **12" DeWalt Sliding Compound Miter Saw with Stand**

» **DeWalt 12" Table Saw**

» **DeWalt Disc Sander**

» **DeWalt 12-Volt Drill/Driver and Impact Driver**

» **Kreg Jig**

» **DeWalt Jigsaw**

» **DeWalt 18-Volt Cordless Finish Nailer with finish nails**

Now that you are geared up with the project key and a list of our favorite tools (even some motivational speeches), roll up your sleeves and let's get going!

Before and After

There isn't anything more exciting than a good before and after. The best ones are furniture makeovers done in one afternoon, simple updates like sprucing up hardware or bringing new life to objects long forgotten. I love a good shoe, but I gotta tell you, seeing the words "reveal" or "makeover" or "before and after" in the title of a new post from my favorite home decor blogs, well, my heart goes pitter-patter. In this chapter, you'll find amazing before and after projects, like a hand-me-down dresser painted two ways, painted countertops, and a table transformed with duct tape. More than anything, I hope you'll be inspired to see that, with a little bit of elbow grease, paint, or creativity, you can change almost anything.

HANDY HOW-TO

Use a smooth nylon brush with an angled edge to work around trim and molding. Using a great brush is the secret to an incredibly smooth finish. P.S. Only paint non-food prep countertop surfaces, as a waxed finish might not seal well enough to avoid bacterial contamination.

Painted Laminate Countertops

If you are like me, there is probably at least one surface in your home you wish you could easily change. If you're not crazy about the pattern and color of your counters, you can easily redo them with this instant makeover. Painting is an affordable and beautiful option, although it's best for low traffic areas. The white wax used in this project can also be easily touched up (if nicked) by reapplying wax with your finger and a soft cloth. You will want to rub the wax on and then rub it in, buffing in a circular motion as you go. The wax should feel almost dry when you are finished applying. This project is fast and makes such a big impact!

COST: $50
DIFFICULTY: ★
TIME: 2 hours

You Will Need:

» Two 4-ounce samples of Annie Sloan Chalk Paint in French Linen
» Nylon angled paintbrush
» Smooth, lint-free cloths or old T-shirts for waxing
» Miss Mustard Seed's White Wax

1. Wipe your counters clean with a damp cloth or a cleaning wipe. Allow it to dry. Don't overthink this step—a quick swipe will do.

2. Paint two coats of the French Linen paint, allowing time for each coat to dry. Chalk paint is fast drying, so this will be quick! Each coat should take approximately 30 minutes or less to dry.

3. Once both coats of paint are dry, rub on the white wax with the smooth cloth. Think of it as spreading on car wax . . . wipe it on, then wipe it off, until it appears smooth to the eye and to the touch. Wax on, wax off.

Marble Paper Countertops

$ COST: $30
DIFFICULTY: ★★
TIME: 1 hour

You Will Need:

» **Measuring tape**
» **Contact paper in Carrera Marble**
  (or other pattern of your choice)
» **Scissors**
» **X-ACTO knife**

Changing kitchen and desk countertops is a dream for many of us, including me. While I'm striving to be content, I decided to make over the desk portion of our kitchen counters using this marble look-a-like contact paper. While four hands are definitely required for this project, it's a relatively easy and very inexpensive way to get a whole new look for your counters. The contact paper is easy to remove and reposition, and it has a soft glossy finish just like real marble. You can choose this pattern, Carrera Marble, or browse many others at *www.designyourwall.com*. This treatment is best for non-food prep surfaces, as a wax treatment might not be 100 percent food safe.

1. Measure any trim or sides and tackle those small strips first, working in sections.

2. Measure the size of the piece you will need to cover the surface. You'll want enough to lay over the edge, so leave excess for that.

3. Cut the piece to size. Start at the corner and have one person hold the contact paper in place while the other gently pulls away the backing as you work.

4. Press the paper down as you go, working out bubbles and wrinkles.

5. Fold any excess under the front, and trim any from the sides with an X-ACTO knife.

If you get a little bubble or wrinkle here and there, don't fret. You can pop a bubble by pressing the point tip of the X-ACTO into it and smoothing the contact paper. The bubble will disappear!

Duct Tape End Table

Duct tape: It's used on everything. We use it to repair rips and tears, to secure, and even to replace windows. Now with new trendy designs, duct tape is more sought after than ever by quick-fix DIYers. The LACK end table from IKEA only costs seven bucks, and you can assemble it in a few minutes while you watch your favorite show. Your table-turned-desk will be perfect for many spaces, and the funky patterned tape will infuse personality into any corner of your home.

COST: $16
DIFFICULTY: ★
TIME: 1 Hour

You Will Need:

» **LACK end table from IKEA** (or another similar table)
» **1 roll of patterned Duck brand duct tape**
» **Scissors**
» **X-ACTO knife**

1. Assemble table, if required.

2. Starting at the top of each leg, press tape onto surface. You'll want to leave a little extra at the top; don't worry, we'll trim that later.

3. Once the tape is straight, pull out and down, securing as you go. Trim tape at the bottom with scissors. Use an X-ACTO knife to trim the top piece so that it's right under the lip of the tabletop.

4. Repeat on every side of all four legs.

Have Fun with Hardware

You Will Need:

- » Hardware
- » Screwdriver
- » Pliers to remove old hardware
  (optional)
- » Drill and bit for new hardware holes
  (optional)
- » Fine or medium-grit sanding sponge
  (optional)
- » Wood putty or spackle (optional)
- » Putty knife (optional)
- » Paint matching the current finish
  (optional)

Hi, my name is Shaunna, and I'm addicted to pretty hardware. I have been known to buy hardware anyplace, anytime. There is no more affordable or simple way to update your furniture or cabinets. Consider what you want the piece to feel like when finished, and be choosy; there are a million options and price points. The point is not to stare at the hardware, but to appreciate the style of the work. From glass to ceramic, bone, and wood, a sizable stash of hardware is a staple for anytime inspiration!

1. Begin by removing the old hardware. Unscrew the bolt on the inside of the drawer with your hand or a screwdriver. If you are having a hard time removing the old hardware, you may need to use pliers to grip the bolt while you turn the knob on the front of the drawer.

2. You can simply replace with hardware that matches the existing holes, but if you wish to change the hardware holes (from a drawer pull to a knob, or vice versa), lightly sand the current holes. Using a putty knife, fill the hole with wood filler or spackle. Press the filler down into the hole, scraping off the top with the putty knife to keep the filler level with the surface. Let the filler dry for approximately 30 minutes.

 3. Lightly sand the hole with a fine or medium sanding sponge, and fill the hole again, making sure to level the top off so the hole is perfectly smooth. Let the second coat dry for approximately 30 minutes.

 4. Lightly sand the holes again, making sure that your putty is completely flush with the surrounding surface.

 5. Measure and drill the new holes with a drill and bit.

6. Touch up the paint of the area you've worked on, if necessary. The former hardware holes should not be seen anymore. Attach your new hardware!

Chippy Milk Paint Wardrobe

Milk paint is probably not for the perfectionist. It is a just-go-with-it kind of paint, and that's the beauty in its finish. This paint does something very special on time-worn pieces. It is unpredictable, though, and sometimes chips or sticks. But overall, it is simple to apply, and it's totally VOC free. Don't balk at the mixing step; it's not difficult at all, just takes some practice to get consistency correct. Treat it like pancake batter: You want it loose, but not too runny. For this piece, you'll want some chipping and wearing through to another color on the drawer fronts, so we'll use two different resist techniques to keep the paint from adhering in those places. If you stick with it, milk paint will give you the kind of finish that appears original to the piece.

COST: $47
DIFFICULTY: ★★
TIME: 2 hours

You Will Need:

» Wardrobe or armoire
» Fine/medium-grit sanding block
» 4-ounce sample of Annie Sloan Chalk Paint in Duck Egg
» Nylon angle paintbrush
» 1 tablespoon of Miss Mustard Seed's Hemp Oil
» Wax puck or tea light candle
» Miss Mustard Seed's Milk Paint in French Enamel (about 1 cup)
» Miss Mustard Seed's Furniture Wax
» Lint-free cloths

1. Dust furniture with a damp cloth or paper towel. If the surface has a glossy finish, scuff it with a medium-grit sanding block so the wood peeking through the finish won't be too shiny.

2. Paint one coat of Duck Egg chalk paint on the drawer fronts and door facing. Let dry.

3. To create the chipping effect, dip your fingers in the hemp oil and then blot them on the surface of the drawers and facing. Think about where the paint would wear naturally: on corners, edges, and near hardware. To create a different kind of resist, run the wax puck or candle along edges and molding.

4. Mix the milk paint powder in French Enamel with water according to instructions (and our pancake batter tip). You will need approximately one cup per coat, and this piece only has one coat.

5. Once the hemp oil and/or wax is in place, paint a topcoat of French Enamel onto the drawers and doors. You'll want to paint it pretty quickly after applying the oil, so the oiled (and/or waxed) areas will "resist" the second coat of paint.

6. Paint one smooth coat of French Enamel on the sides, trim, and body of the armoire. Repeat resist on the feet, trim, or edges if desired. Let dry.

7. After the piece has completely dried, buff off the places where a resist was used with a smooth cloth or a fine/medium-grit sanding block. Distress any other edges. A note on distressing: The point is to see the furniture, not the distressing. A little goes a long way, and when distressing heavily, choose a few hot spots and let those steal the show so that you don't create a spotted dresser.

8. Wipe away any dust from distressing.

9. Wipe on a coat of furniture wax with a brush or cloth, and wipe it off with another cloth as you go. The furniture should feel barely damp or tacky when finished. Let dry. Revel in the beauty of your milk paint goodness.

HANDY HOW-TO

I love the colors of Miss Mustard Seed's Milk Paint, and I prefer the powder form. General Finishes Milk Paint is another powder option. Start mixing by wetting the powder until all of the liquid is absorbed. Continue adding water a teaspoon at a time, stirring gently with a stir stick. Mix gently for about 5–7 minutes, until the paint is more creamy than lumpy.

Hand-Me-Down Dresser, Chalk Paint Finish

COST: $20
DIFFICULTY: ★
TIME: 45 minutes

You Will Need:

- » Dresser
- » Tools for removing hardware
- » Smooth cloth
- » Nylon angled paintbrush
- » Annie Sloan Chalk Paint in Napoleonic Blue (about 1 cup)

We all have those pieces that have been passed down to us through the years. Some are simple chests or tables or chairs that can be replaced over time. But some of them . . . some of them stick with you. We can't quite let them go. I have this rule in my house: If I love it and I want it to stay, the piece has to remain relevant. Sometimes refinishing is in order, and other times a fresh coat of paint gives a piece's outdated finish the new life it needs. You'll see how very different the same dresser can look—from rustic cottage, to feminine and glamorous—and how easy it is to completely transform one of your own pieces.

 Remove the hardware, and wipe the dresser off with a smooth cloth to remove any dust.

 Using the nylon brush, paint on a thin coat of Napoleonic Blue chalk paint. Don't be too particular, as this paint is very forgiving, and the wood peeking out underneath is just the right rustic touch. Let dry for approximately thirty minutes.

3. Once the first coat is dry, smooth the paint finish by buffing with a cloth, using a circular motion.

4. Leave the chunky knobs or other hardware in their original state and put them back on the chest.

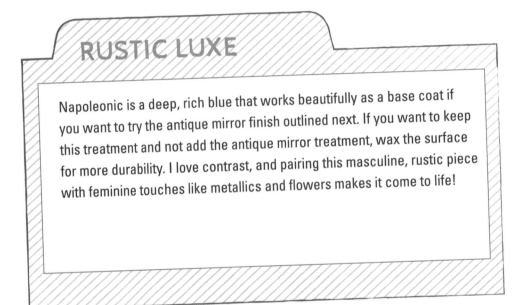

RUSTIC LUXE

Napoleonic is a deep, rich blue that works beautifully as a base coat if you want to try the antique mirror finish outlined next. If you want to keep this treatment and not add the antique mirror treatment, wax the surface for more durability. I love contrast, and pairing this masculine, rustic piece with feminine touches like metallics and flowers makes it come to life!

Hand-Me-Down Dresser, Antique Mirror Finish

Metallics have made a comeback. You'll no longer only find metallic and mirrored furniture in the swankiest homes, but also in feminine cottages, traditional abodes, and dorm rooms alike. The beauty of a mirrored finish is that it's completely neutral, the perfect complement for an elegant bedroom or a farmhouse entryway. Choosing your base coat for this treatment is key. Think about an antiqued mirror—this dresser wouldn't have the same appeal with red showing through. Deep navy, charcoal, black, or a chocolate brown are your best bets for achieving your own antiqued mirror finish.

COST: $24
DIFFICULTY: ★★
TIME: 1½ hours

You Will Need:

» **Dresser** (painted; see previous project)
» **Drop cloth**
» **Krylon Premium Metallic Spray in Silver Foil**
» **Spray leaf adhesive**
» **Silver or aluminum leaf sheets** (found in craft stores)
» **Chip brush** (a flat, inexpensive brush found at home improvement stores)

1. Remove hardware and drawers from body of the dresser to make painting easier. You don't have to do this if you're strapped for time, but it's the best way to get a smooth, drip-free finish.

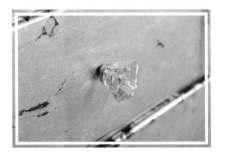

2. Spray the body and top of the dresser with the Silver Foil metallic spray, sweeping in fluid motions. Let dry for approximately thirty minutes.

3. Some sprays require time to get tacky, but if you use this brand you can start leafing the drawers right away. Working in sections, spray on the adhesive.

4. Carefully remove the leaf sheet from the pack, trying to keep it as intact as possible. Place it on top of the adhesive.

5. Using your chip brush, burnish (a fancy word for "press") the silver leaf onto the tacky spots. Don't be too particular; part of the charm and look of an antiqued mirror finish is chipping, so bits of the blue base coat peeking out are a must. Your imperfection is doing this dresser a favor!

6. Repeat the burnishing until all drawer fronts are covered. Let this piece sit untouched for a day or two, then buff with a smooth cloth and replace the hardware. You can finish off with wipe-on polyurethane, but this piece will be durable as is. Plus, a little chipping in the future will only enhance the look.

HANDY HOW-TO

The trick with spray finishes is to apply two or three thin, smooth coats. Start spraying an inch or so above the surface of the dresser, sweep the spray in a straight line, stop spraying, then repeat. No back and forth or side-to-side motions, if you want to avoid a streaky mess.

Modern Yellow Buffet

You Will Need:

» Lint-free cloths or old T-shirt

» Annie Sloan Chalk Paint in English Yellow (about ¼ of quart can)

» Nylon angled paintbrush

» Small bowl of water

» 600-grit sandpaper (available online or specialty hardware stores) or a super-fine sanding block

» Annie Sloan Soft Wax in Clear

» Wax brush (optional)

» New hardware (optional)

If you're a little shy with color, it might scare you to death to paint something in such a bold hue. You know what, though? There is a little secret about paint: You can always paint right back over it again. Bright colors look the best on clean, sharp lines, and this straight, retro buffet, complete with fans on the front, looks amazing in this bold yellow. Use this rule when painting your own furniture: Straight and simple can pull off bold color, while curvy and ornate look best in layered finishes or simple creams, whites, and grays, with some distressing and antiquing.

1. Wipe your piece free of dust and start painting. To create the smoothest finish, dip your brush in water, then into the paint to thin it a little.

2. Let dry, then paint a second coat. Keep in mind we're going for a sleek finish, so paint in any direction, but don't lay down too much paint as you apply. See a tutorial video on my blog at *www.perfectly imperfectblog.com/ the50homemakeover*!

3. Using the sandpaper, lightly sand in a circular motion. We're smoothing the brushstrokes and the paint, not distressing, so keep that in mind as you apply pressure.

 4. Buff the piece with a cloth. Chalk paint is very, well, chalky, so buff away any dust with a circular motion.

 5. Apply clear wax with a rag or brush, and have a clean rag ready for buffing as you apply. This will create a buttery finish, and it hardens the paint to protect your piece. Finish it off with funky hardware!

HANDY HOW-TO

We're creating a smooth, modern look, so choose your piece accordingly. You probably can't recreate this look on a curvy, beaten-up table, so go with the clean lines of a piece that's in pretty great shape and requires little prep.

Layered Antique Dresser

I'm a big believer in painting old furniture. Yes, even the pieces your grandmother gave you. Your home should be filled with items you love and cherish, and that are relevant to you now. If you adore timeworn wood, then don't paint it. But if that piece in the corner is bothering you, yet the thought of painting it scares you to death, this treatment is a great option. Think of it as accentuating the beauty of it without completely covering the wood. Go on, look around your house right now. I know there's a piece calling for this simple treatment!

$ COST: $45
DIFFICULTY: ★★
TIME: 2 hours

You Will Need:

» **Chest of drawers**
» **Medium-grit sanding block**
» **Water**
» **1 cup of white paint** (latex, acrylic, chalk paint, or milk paint will do)
» **Angled nylon paintbrush**
» **3–5 smooth cloths**
» **Furniture wax or Minwax Wipe-On Poly** (or other wipe-on polyurethane finish)

1. Rough the surface of your piece with a sanding block. Don't apply too much pressure; you don't want to scratch the surface. Sand in a circular motion, paying attention to the flat areas like the top, sides, and drawer fronts. Wipe any dust off the chest.

2. Fill a cup with about ¾ cup of water and ¼ cup white paint and stir it up well to make a wash. To get the look of the chest illustrated here, use white latex paint.

 3. Dip your brush into the wash, wiping it off along the side of the cup. Working on one section at a time, paint on the wash. Be sure to work it into the details, allowing the white to settle.

4. Fold a clean cloth so that the surface is smooth, and wipe the wash off as you apply it. Remember to work in sections. For example, apply the wash to all of one side, and wipe it off there before moving on to paint the top. Wipe until the wash is smooth and seamless. The point is to create a sheer "film," not paint on a solid color.

5. Repeat the wash as many times as necessary, allowing it to dry in between coats. The dresser illustrated has two coats of the wash.

6. Dry-brush some white onto the highlights (details) of the dresser. This will pull the eye to the beautiful woodwork. Use a light hand and add several dry brushed "layers" instead of putting on too much paint at once. Dry-brush by dipping your brush lightly in paint, and squeezing off excess with a cloth. The brush should feel almost dry, with little paint, as you highlight the raised curves.

7. Wax your dresser to seal in the hard work. Using a brush or cloth, wipe the wax on the dresser, and wipe off as you go with another smooth cloth. Rub in circular motions to create sheen.

This treatment looks great on almost any piece of furniture, but especially those with some detail for the paint to settle into. The more porous and dried out the furniture, the better.

Dry-Brushed Laundry Door

You Will Need:

» FrogTape or painter's tape
» Smooth angled nylon sash brush
» Flat latex paint
» Paper towels
» Minwax Wipe-On Poly (optional)

Do you have an all-neutral or boring color palette? Do all of your doors and trim match exactly? Maybe it's time for a quick update. Painting the perfectly placed door can make such a statement in corners of your home. Look around, and see what little nook could use a pop of color and personality.

1. Choose a door to paint. Think about painting a powder room door, or the door to the laundry or pantry—any area in your home that could use a little color. There's no need to remove the door. If you'd like, tape off the hardware with FrogTape.

2. Dip your angled sash brush in a little paint, and squeeze the excess paint into a paper towel, so the brush is almost dry as you paint. This allows the original color to peek out underneath your new hue. Paint in the grooves and details first. When painting around the hinges, press the brush flatter so the angled edge spreads and lets you cut in around the hardware.

3. After painting the details, paint the flat surfaces. As you paint, you can use the dry-brush technique in certain spots so the door isn't fully coated, or you can choose to paint two smooth coats.

4. Latex paint is self-sealing, so it doesn't need a topcoat. If you'd like a little shine, apply a coat of Minwax Wipe-On Poly (or other wipe-on polyurethane) in a satin finish with a sponge or rag.

Take your makeover a step further by replacing the doorknob with a knock-off antique knob or another funky choice from your favorite store.

HANDY HOW-TO

When painting details and small patterns, treat your paintbrush like a pencil. Use less paint and try to "write" onto the trim. Also keep in mind that the flatter you spread a small angled brush, the more you can create a straight edge.

Painted Details

So many pieces are *almost* right. They have great lines or interesting character, and they don't need a full paint job. Or, hey, sometimes your budget just doesn't allow for a full furniture makeover. Painting the details provides the same impact, but gives you lots of bang for your buck. This treatment is best for pieces of furniture that are filled with carving, moldings, or curves.

1. Wipe your piece off to remove any dust or crumbs. (We get a *lot* of both in our house.)

2. Using a medium craft paintbrush, paint one coat of Apricot Ice (or the lighter color of your choices) onto the inset of the drawer front.

3. Move on to the molding (or raised details). Using the small paintbrush, paint on the Amber Rose (or your chosen darker color). Be flexible, and don't worry about perfect lines. You won't notice once it's finished. Keep baby wipes handy to wipe any mistakes as you go.

4. Repeat with a second coat of the darker color if needed.

COST: $5
DIFFICULTY: ★
TIME: 30 minutes

You Will Need:

» **Any piece of furniture with raised and inset detailing**

» **Craft paintbrushes, medium and very small**

» **Sample pot(s) of latex paint** (this table used Valspar's Apricot Ice and Amber Rose)

» **Baby wipes**

Whitewash Lamp

- 💰 **COST:** $40
- 🛠 **DIFFICULTY:** ★
- ⏱ **TIME:** 30 minutes

You Will Need:

» **Cup for mixing paint wash**

» **White paint** (latex, acrylic, or Annie Sloan Chalk Paint—this lamp uses Annie Sloan Chalk Paint in Pure White)

» **Angled nylon paintbrush or natural hair chip brush**

» **Carved wood lamp**

» **Clean lint-free cloths**

You are probably like me—you don't want to spend $300 for one lamp. Keep your eyes peeled not only at thrift stores, but at big-box stores like Target, Hobby Lobby, World Market, and Walmart. If you love the shape and the price, grab it, then take it home and paint it!

1. Fill a cup with about ¾ cup of water and ¼ cup white paint and stir it up well.

2. Lightly dab the wash into the grooves of your lamp using a gentle bouncing motion, wiping drips as you go.

3. After painting the wash on one side, feather the wash off with your cloth. Think of feathering as simply lightly wiping, so you don't remove the entire wash. Remember that you're working with wood, a more porous material, so you won't want the paint to sit for a long time. One to two minutes is enough.

4. Repeat this on all four sides of the lamp, paying attention to the corners: smooth them where the wash might create lines.

HANDY HOW-TO

For a wash to look seamless, work in sections and always use a light hand when wiping and smoothing the paint. Think of it as feathering with your cloth instead of wiping hard. This will smooth lines and blend hard edges and paint drips.

Painted Builder-Grade Cabinets

We all have cabinets that we like, but don't love; cabinets that are oak, or worn, or, in our case, blah. I love white cabinetry, but we have it all over our home, and this little bathroom was begging for some personality and depth. You can read more about the full room makeover on our blog (*www.perfectlyimperfectblog.com/2013/10/cottage-guest-bathroom-reveal.html*), but this tutorial will show you how simple it is to paint those lackluster boxes you have all over your home and transform them into something special.

This is one of those projects you will be thrilled that you tackled. But you must resist the urge to run guests immediately into your bathroom to brag about your beautiful cabinetry. (Ahem.)

COST: $30
DIFFICULTY: ★
TIME: 3 hours

You Will Need:

- » 1 cup Annie Sloan Chalk Paint in Paris Grey
- » Nylon angled paintbrush (such as a Purdy XL Cub)
- » ½ cup Annie Sloan Chalk Paint in Pure White
- » ½ cup of water
- » Annie Sloan Soft Wax
- » Clean lint-free cloths
- » New hardware

1. Remove the hardware from your cabinet, but you can keep the doors on. Next, paint two coats of Paris Grey, allowing dry time in between.

2. After the second coat of grey dries, mix up a 50:50 ratio of Pure White paint to water.

3. Apply the wash, working it into the grooves first, then onto the flat surfaces. Wipe it as you go, smoothing lines and drips. Stop painting at the edge of the cabinet opening. I don't paint the inside of my cabinets, but you could if you would like to.

4. After the topcoat of wash dries, rub on the soft wax to seal it. As you apply the wax, wipe it in and buff with another smooth cloth. Put on your new hardware!

WHERE TO FIND IT

When painting your cabinets, decided what look you're going for. If you simply want a smooth, white finish, go for oil-based or latex enamel and primer. It's self-sealing and won't require any waxing. If you want more of a layered or timeworn finish, go for the no-priming-or-sanding quality of chalk paint.

Chalkboard Table

Ah, chalkboard paint . . . endless fun and contained coloring. This project took a total of 15 minutes after this IKEA table was put together by my handy husband. Almost any surface can be painted with chalkboard paint, and because it has such a matte finish, it adheres well to prefab surfaces like this tabletop. The LATT table and chair set only cost $19.99 for all three pieces, and the top slides in as you build, making it the perfect candidate for spraying beforehand. You could shop around thrift stores and flea markets for a table like this, too. Small children's tables and chairs or even old school desks are just right for your little artists' very own chalkboard.

COST: $30
DIFFICULTY: ★
TIME: 15 minutes

You Will Need:

» **LATT set of table and chairs from IKEA** (or a similar table)
» **Drop cloth**
» **½ can chalkboard spray paint**
» **Chalk**

1. Put the table together according to the directions, but keep the top separate. Spray it with a thin coat of chalkboard paint, using a smooth sweeping motion. Allow it to dry until dry to the touch. Paint drying times vary depending on humidity and how thick the paint coat is.

2. Paint the top with two more thin coats, allowing dry time in between.

3. Once the top has dried overnight, bring it back to your table. Season it by rubbing the long side of the chalk (not the end) all over the surface. This step is essential. Otherwise you'll just scratch the surface of your board.

4. Slide the top into your table and finish assembling it. Write and draw away!

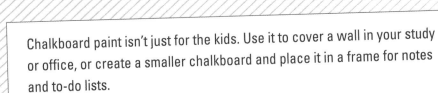

STYLE FILE

Chalkboard paint isn't just for the kids. Use it to cover a wall in your study or office, or create a smaller chalkboard and place it in a frame for notes and to-do lists.

Gold Leaf and Faux Marble Coffee Table

by Kristin Hunter of *The Hunted Interior*

I'm Kristin, and I'm an interior designer and the writer behind *The Hunted Interior*. With a background in international hotel design, I know the importance of thinking outside of the box, creating luxurious spaces, and making every dollar count.

After seeing some of the hottest coffee tables around (with prices to match), I decided I could create my own high-end look on a budget anyone can afford. By simply applying a layer of gold leaf and creating a faux marble base, I took this table from a recognizable big-box-store look to a "where did you get that?!" look. While this project isn't under $50, you could easily repurpose a table or use a flea market find instead of buying the $60 IKEA tables.

COST: $40 with repurposed table, $100 as shown

DIFFICULTY: ★★★

TIME: 2½ hours

You Will Need:

» **Spray adhesive**

» **Table(s)**, such as the VITTSJÖ nesting tables from IKEA

» **Gold leaf**

» **Gold leaf or acrylic sealer spray**

» **White latex primer**

» **Feather or torn piece of cardboard**

» **2" nylon paintbrush**

» **Black craft paint**

» **Damp rag**

» **Furniture wax or wax sealer**

 1. Apply spray adhesive to the legs a small section at a time, and lay on the individual sheets of gold leaf. Press the sheets down with your fingers. They do not need to be laid perfectly straight, as a little crack in the gold leaf looks more authentic, like aged metal.

 2. Once the table is covered and gorgeous, spray two or three layers of gold leaf sealer to protect your hard work.

 3. Using the 2" brush, paint the base of the table with the primer and allow it to dry. Once this is dry, add another layer.

4. While the second layer of primer is still wet, dip your feather (or torn piece of cardboard) into the black craft paint. Drag the feather through the wet primer, twisting your wrist as you go. This helps to give the veining effect prominent in marble.

5. Feather out the veining, using either your damp rag or a dry brush. To feather, simply lightly slide your brush or cloth along the paint line to soften the edges.

6. Continue to layer on primer (or any white latex paint) and add more veins until the look you desire is achieved. Quickly but gently dabbing the surface with a damp rag in a straight up-and-down motion helps to give the surface a natural stone finish instead of a painted look.

7. After you are satisfied with your design, simply seal with a few coats of furniture wax. The wax gives the "marble" a truer honed look.

HANDY HOW-TO

There are no two identical slabs of marble in the world, so feel free to play around with your marble effects. If I am feeling stuck, I like to print out a few examples of marble and use those as inspiration. The more layers you add, the more authentic it will look.

Painted Stool

COST: $10
DIFFICULTY: ★
TIME: 20 minutes

You Will Need:

» Drop cloth
» Stool or small piece of furniture
» Little people to do the painting
» Up to 3 colors of acrylic paint
» Small paintbrushes
» FrogTape (optional)

These little stools are great to help small feet. You don't have to spend a fortune on pieces like this. Small items are the perfect way to repurpose or reinvent your way to a budget-friendly home. Can't find one at a flea market? Grab one you like from a discount store and paint it that afternoon, or, even better, let your little ones give it a makeover. Much like for the Kid Wall Art Gallery later in the book, I gave my kids three colors and one rule: Don't get paint on my floor.

1. Spread your drop cloth on the floor or table. Give each child a color of paint and a brush—they can always swap later. It saves time if you pass out the colors yourself. Promise.

2. Let them paint while you have a cup of coffee. The more splatters, the better. Anything you don't want paint on, tape up.

3. To recreate the two-tone look, simply give them one color at a time. We used the blue paint first, then the green. This creates a layered, smeared look. If you like, tape along the top edge to avoid drips or running paint.

Don't feel like the kids can only paint a stool. Let them try their hands at painting a small end table or a chair for their rooms.

HANDY HOW-TO

It's okay if the tape gets a few wrinkles in it. Keep working with it and take your time. And you know what? Live with a little wrinkle if it is being stubborn.

Washi Tape Drawer Fronts

The beauty of this taped drawer front project is this: It's *tape*. You can apply these pretty patterned tapes to almost anything; they will go on quickly and you can remove them easily.

COST: $7
DIFFICULTY: ☆
TIME: 10 minutes

 1. Start at one end of your drawer and press the tape down into one corner of the drawer front.

 2. Gently pull the tape, smoothing it down as you go. It is much easier to pull directly from the roll rather than cutting and placing an entire piece at once.

 3. Continue pulling until you press the last bit of tape into the corner of the opposite end.

4. Trim away excess. Be careful not to scratch your furniture; the X-ACTO blade should be sharp enough to cut the tape with very little pressure.

 5. Repeat until the drawer front is covered with washi tape. Repeat with each drawer.

You Will Need:

» Chest of drawers or other piece of furniture
» Wide washi tape
» X-ACTO knife

IKEA RAST, *Grey Weathered Stain*

💲 **COST:** $45

🔨 **DIFFICULTY:** ★

⏱ **TIME:** 1 hour

You Will Need:

» IKEA RAST chest

» 2 staining pads or foam brush

» Rust-Oleum Grey Weathered Stain

» Minwax Wipe-On Poly in satin finish, or clear wax

The RAST chest from **IKEA** is a blank slate. It's literally a box, with simple wooden knobs. You can take this basic piece from Plain Jane to modern, cottage-chic, or traditional. You can add new hardware, metal trim, beautiful wood molding, or even unfinished furniture feet. Feel free to add your own personality to it, and use as a chest, end table, or bedside table. The possibilities are truly endless with these little guys.

1. Assemble your chest of drawers according to the instructions. Leave the hardware off and leave the drawers separate from the body.

2. Using a staining pad or foam brush, rub a thin coat of the stain on your piece, rubbing in every direction so that the grain fully accepts the stain.

3. Let the stain sit for three minutes or so. With another staining pad, rub the stain in while wiping the excess off.

4. Seal your little chest with Minwax Wipe-On Poly or a clear wax. Replace the hardware, or stain the wooden knobs if you'd like everything to match.

Test stains yourself instead of relying on the swatch at the store or on the strip. Stains look completely different on each type of wood, and many swatches show a more opaque coat. We tend to use one coat of stain to create sheer coats that allow the grain to shine.

IKEA RAST, *Milk Paint and Paper*

You Will Need:

» IKEA RAST chest
» Miss Mustard Seed's Milk Paint in Artissimo
» Nylon paintbrush
» Miss Mustard Seed's Hemp Oil Wood Finish
» Smooth cloth
» Krylon Gold Metallic Spray Paint
» Measuring tape
» Scissors or X-ACTO knife
» Heavy weight decoupage paper, gift-wrap, wallpaper, or scrapbook paper
» Foam brush
» Mod Podge or decoupage paste

This tutorial will show you how extremely different this piece can become with richly hued milk paint and some papered drawers. Milk paint works beautifully on raw wood; the paint soaks into the wood so it adheres really well. If you love to see the wood grain, stick to one coat. But if you would like a more opaque finish, two to three coats are best. In this makeover, you will also get to play with decoupage and decorative papers to line the drawers. The inside of the drawers are where you can really add some punch to your design.

1. Assemble your piece according to the instructions. Remove the drawers so you can paint the insides and the frame easily.

2. Mix the Artissimo paint powder with water according to instructions on the package until smooth. The paint is like pancake batter—the more you stir, the more smoothly mixed the powder and water become. You will need approximately one cup per coat. Feel free to make the paint a little runnier, since the raw wood will soak it up quickly.

3. Paint one smooth coat onto the piece, including the inside frame and inside drawers. Let dry for approximately thirty minutes.

4. Apply the hemp oil topcoat with a smooth cloth or foam brush. Hemp oil soaks into the wood, so wipe away any excess after about ten minutes.

5. Spray two thin coats of gold spray paint onto the wooden knobs. Be sure to turn them over to cover hard-to-reach areas.

6. Measure the bottom inside of one drawer. Cut paper to size with scissors or an X-ACTO knife.

7. Using your foam brush, brush Mod Podge onto the back of your paper or the bottom of the drawer. Quickly but carefully, place the paper into the drawer. Line up the edges in one corner and press the paper down.

8. Immediately apply a topcoat of Mod Podge to the paper. This will cause little bubbles and wrinkles, but don't worry, those will disappear when the paste is dry. Reapply additional topcoats every hour, allowing the paste to dry in between coats. You can stick to only one topcoat, but additional coats will add more shine and durability.

9. Reattach your shiny gold knobs to the piece and enjoy it!

STYLE FILE

If you decide you don't want to use paper to cover the bottom of the drawers, you can always add personality to a piece by painting the insides of a drawer a complementary or contrasting color. Pair greys with rich blues, aqua, or red; whites with anything; and soft creams with gray-greens, navy, or even coral.

IKEA RAST, Latex Paint Finish

COST: $50
DIFFICULTY: ★
TIME: 30 minutes

You Will Need:

» **IKEA RAST chest**
» **Nylon paintbrush**
» **Latex paint sample** (this piece uses Pantone Universe for Lowe's in Emerald)
» **Furniture knobs** (optional)

While I love a hand-painted look, there is nothing prettier than a lustrous latex finish. You can pick up inexpensive sample pots of latex paint at your local home improvement store that will easily cover a small piece of furniture. The beauty of latex paint is that is durable and self-sealing, requiring no topcoat.

1. Assemble your piece according to the instructions. Remove the drawers so you can easily reach all the parts of the chest.

2. Paint a thin coat of latex paint onto the entire piece, including the insides if you'd like them painted. As you paint, be sure to use long, fluid motions. Allow a couple of hours of dry time to ensure it dries well, then paint another thin coat.

3. Allow to dry for 24 hours, then add your hardware!

HANDY HOW-TO

If you'd like more shine to your finish, try using a high-gloss polyurethane finish. Apply two hours after your final coat of paint.

French Reproduction Table

If you look around in furniture stores, and even some chain home goods retailers, you will run across some reproduction pieces like this little hallway table. I love buying solid wood antiques as much as anyone, but these pieces are just as beautiful and they come at a fraction of the price. Chances are you already have a piece like this, handed down from your mother or relative, just as we did. You can leave these pieces as-is, or you can create a layered finish that mimics those gorgeous painted antiques.

COST: $25
DIFFICULTY: ★★★
TIME: 1½ hours

You Will Need:

» Curvy or carved table
» Annie Sloan Chalk Paint in Duck Egg
» 2 natural bristle paintbrushes
» Annie Sloan Chalk Paint in French Linen
» Fine-grit sanding block
» Lint-free cloths
» Miss Mustard Seed's White Wax

1. Paint one thick coat of Duck Egg on your table. Be sure to dab your brush in all the curves and details of the piece. Let dry.

2. Slightly dampen another brush with water. This will make your topcoat of French Linen sheer and light, allowing the Duck Egg to peek out from underneath.

3. As you paint the topcoat of French Linen around the details, lighten your pressure so you don't completely cover the Duck Egg. Lightly sweep the brush back and forth around those areas instead of pressing the paint on. Slightly swipe your brush over the details, allowing the Duck Egg to continue peeking out. Allow the topcoat to dry.

4. Distress the table along the edges and the curves with the sanding block. Vary your pressure so that sometimes you reveal the pretty blue/green underneath, and sometimes you distress right down to the wood.

5. Once you've distressed to your liking, wipe away any dust with a cloth. With a lint-free cloth, rub and lightly dab on the white wax. Be sure to let the white wax gather in the grooves and carved details. This will create a gathering of the wax in the grooves, highlighting the carving. Wipe off the excess white wax from the flat surfaces as you go, and buff the top slightly as you rub the wax in. This will create some luster and shine.

HANDY HOW-TO

When distressing, keep in mind that you want to focus on the areas that would wear naturally over time. Rub along edges, corners, and the curve or foot of a leg. This will make your piece look much more naturally worn and aged.

Striped Curtains

Here's one design rule worth remembering: Spend a little more money on the fabric that touches your skin (like bedding, pillows, etc.) and cut corners on the fabric you don't touch (like drapes and shower curtains). Curtains are the perfect place to save some dough. Pair inexpensive neutral panels from IKEA (some as low as only $19.95 per pair!) with a little paint for a unique, striking statement.

COST: $28
DIFFICULTY: ★
TIME: 45 minutes per panel

You Will Need:

» **White curtain panel**
» **Measuring tape**
» **Pencil**
» **FrogTape**
» **Annie Sloan Chalk Paint in French Linen**
» **Martha Stewart Crafts Fabric Medium**
» **Natural bristle paintbrush** (such as an Annie Sloan paintbrush in medium)

1. Wash and iron your curtain panel to remove any prewashed fabric treatment that might prevent paint from adhering. Lay on a flat surface.

2. Measure 8" up from the bottom in several places along the width of the panel, making a mark with your pencil as you go.

3. Place FrogTape directly along the pencil markings. Make sure to press your tape firmly to the fabric to prevent any paint from bleeding through.

4. Once the bottom piece of tape is in place, measure up 10" from the top of the bottom piece of tape (or your desired stripe width) along the width of your fabric. Once again, make pencil markings and firmly press a second piece of FrogTape along them.

5. Mix your paint and fabric medium according to instructions. The fabric medium thins your paint and helps it stick to the fabric.

6. Dab on the paint mix between the pieces of tape to create your stripe. Be sure to paint the fabric in a location with good lighting, so you can see how opaque your application is. Let dry.

7. Hold the curtain up to the light and look for any areas that aren't covered completely. Paint over the stripe again, paying special attention to those areas.

8. Immediately and carefully remove the FrogTape—this prevents any extra paint from pulling off the fabric. Set with an iron within twenty-four hours. Now your curtains are machine-washable.

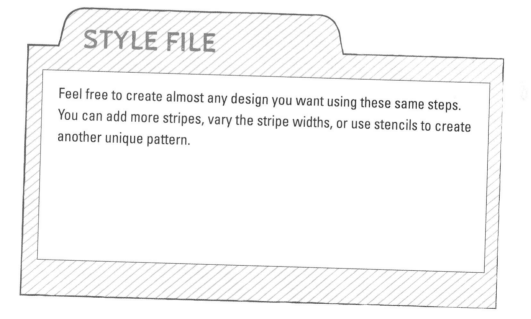

STYLE FILE

Feel free to create almost any design you want using these same steps. You can add more stripes, vary the stripe widths, or use stencils to create another unique pattern.

HANDY HOW-TO

Don't feel like you must measure every single step. You can measure the first step, and after that, simply eyeball the tape placement of the rest of the stair risers.

Washi Tape Striped Steps

Painted stair risers are everywhere in the design world these days. If you love the look but can't quite commit to painting colorful stripes on your stairway, try this easy project. You can transform your stairs with a little creativity, tape, and an X-ACTO knife. Plus, no permanence necessary.

COST: $15
DIFFICULTY: ★
TIME: 2 hours

You Will Need:

» **Measuring tape**
» **4 to 5 rolls of Duck or washi tape** (You will not use an entire roll of any color.)
» **X-ACTO knife**

1. Start on the top step riser. Measure 5" in from the left side of the wall, and place your first color of tape just under the top tread. Don't worry about a perfect line; that is what we will use our X-ACTO for.

2. Press the tape firmly down as you gently pull down toward the bottom of the riser. Try to leave extra tape overlapping onto the next stair tread.

3. Trim the excess on the top and bottom with the X-ACTO knife. Be careful not to scratch your riser; the X-ACTO blade should be sharp enough to cut the tape with very little pressure.

4. Eyeball where you would like your next stripe placed. Repeat the same process for this piece and the rest of your pattern. We used five stripes.

5. Move to the next riser and repeat for each step.

Giftwrap-Backed Bookcase

💲 **COST:** $8–20,

⏲ **DIFFICULTY:** ★

🕐 **TIME:** 1 hour

You Will Need:

» Measuring tape
» Heavyweight matte paper
» Pencil
» X-ACTO knife or scissors
» Matte giftwrap tape

Commitment is hard. We all have those pieces we *just can't paint*. Maybe someone special gave them to us, or maybe we don't want to cover up the wood. Maybe we just can't commit to one color. Either way, this simple project might be for you. Using heavyweight scrapbook or wrapping paper to cover the back panel of a bookcase will lighten the look and add a ton of personality, without having to commit to paint. This is such an affordable, simple project, and it is perfect for apartment dwellers who may not have much painting and crafting space!

1. Measure your shelf backing.

2. Measure those same dimensions on your paper and mark with a pencil. Cut your paper to size with an X-ACTO knife or scissors.

3. Place tape on the wrong side of all four corners and in the middle of the paper. Press onto the furniture, starting at the top corners and pressing down.

4. Repeat on each shelf, and voilà! Style your shelf to your heart's content.

etcetera
etc.

Sibella Cou

BEST LOVED BOOKS

Painted Bed

COST: $25
DIFFICULTY: ★★
TIME: 1½ hours

You Will Need:

» Annie Sloan Chalk Paint in Coco
» Natural bristle paintbrush
» Lint-free cloths
» Miss Mustard Seed's White Wax
» Wax brush or stiff bristle brush

Our bed is huge, one of those big-box store purchases we made immediately after marrying. It's pretty, but it's a little too large for our bedroom, and I have been pining to get rid of it for some time. If you are like us, you probably have a few furniture purchases you now regret. But as I try to teach our children to enjoy what we have and to be content, I realize that I should try to make the best of our bed. What piece of furniture is an eyesore for you? Which room holds that prefabricated piece you can't stand, but can't afford to replace? Try painting it—my bet is you will fall in love with it again.

1. You may want to remove your mattress while painting the bed frame, but if your mattress fits tightly enough that any visible area can be painted, then skip this step.

2. Paint two coats of the Coco, allowing dry time (about 30 minutes for each coat) in between. Press your brush into any details or carvings.

3. Before the paint dries, run a wet cloth over any edges or raised carvings to give them a distressed look. This wet-distress technique will help you avoid dust that you would get from sanding. Using a wet cloth to distress is the best choice since you will probably be painting this piece in your bedroom.

4. Wax the bed with the white wax. Let the white wax collect along the carvings and grooves, wiping the excess away as you go.

5. Apply a second coat of white wax on raised areas to create contrast. The bed pictured has two coats of wax along the flat areas of the headboard, causing the raised panels to stand out in contrast to the rest of the headboard.

CHAPTER 2

Semi–Handmade

If you're anything like me, you gravitate to the simple crafting projects, ones you can complete in a few hours or less. Not many of us have time for weekend-long crafting, and this semi-handmade section is for you. In this section, you'll find loads of simple, fun crafts and projects that even the most anti-crafty folk can tackle. Start with an easy project like dipped flatware, and then progress to the pretty wreaths, or even to painted pillows. But rest assured that none of these projects require "crafting from scratch," fancy supplies, or a ton of work. I promise.

Dip-Dyed Flatware

 COST: $10 for 8 three-piece place settings

DIFFICULTY: ★

TIME: 15 minutes

Dip-dyeing is all the rage in the design world. If you love paint like I do, you'll be excited to try your hand at a simple paint-dipping project. I love stylish and festive entertaining, and this easy dip-dyed birch flatware was tackled in less than 15 minutes.

You Will Need:

» **Waxed paper or parchment paper**

» **Birch flatware** (available online)

» **Sample pot of latex paint** (color of your choice)

» **Small craft brush**

1. Lay out a sheet of waxed or parchment paper for drying your flatware.

2. Dip the handle of each utensil in the paint sample pot, letting excess drip off before laying it onto the wax paper.

3. Walk away and take a nap. Seriously, you're done.

HANDY HOW-TO

Latex paint isn't food safe, so you won't want to use this at a kids' party. If you want something kid-safe, you could always dye the flatware with a fruit and vegetable puree. Or you could just save the dipped flatware for the grown-up parties. These are disposable, so toss them when you're done!

Simple Reclaimed Wooden Placemat

COST: $5–7
DIFFICULTY: ★★
TIME: 1 hour

You Will Need:

» **Table saw or circular saw** (optional, see instructions)
» **One 2' × 2' sheet of ¼" thick birch plywood** (to be cut into 12" × 20" placemats)
» **Wood glue**
» **Package of 12" wood shims**
» **Clamps, or a couple of heavy stacks of books**
» **Staining pad**
» **Stain** (such as Minwax Dark Walnut)

In any home decor style, adding the warmth and texture of reclaimed or worn wood can make such a difference. As beautiful as white is, it's nothing without the balance of wood tones and texture. These placemats are perfect for a fall or Thanksgiving table. Pair them with mix-and-match thrift store dishes for a completely unique and warm table setting. But do keep in mind that we're not dealing with high quality, stain-grade wood for this placemat, and that's actually perfect. The stain will accept differently on each shim, but that creates depth and variation and mimics reclaimed pieces.

1. With the table saw, cut the 12" × 20" placemats from the birch plywood. (Alternatively, you can have them cut to size at your home improvement store.)

2. Using wood glue, glue the shims to the plywood. For a reclaimed look, alternate laying the wide ends with the narrow ends at the top. Try to line them up just to the edge, but again, it doesn't have to be perfect. We're going for a reclaimed look!

3. Once you've attached the shims with glue, clamp them down or use stacks of books to apply pressure for the glue to set. Leave up to twenty-four hours.

4. Dip the staining pad into the can of stain and spread thinly on the placemat. Let it dry. One coat should be enough, but feel free to apply two if necessary.

HANDY HOW-TO

Remember, this placemat isn't food safe. You can always seal your work with a sealant, such as a Wipe-on Polyurethane, but you still wouldn't want to place food directly on the placemat to serve.

Spring Wreath

You Will Need:

» Scissors or pliers
» Artificial blooms
» Store-bought grapevine wreath
» Craft moss
» Hot glue gun
» Hot glue sticks

People have been creating beautiful wreaths for centuries, and hey, while you might not have time to string together your own branches from the yard, crafting a simple spring wreath is still appealing. This wreath is so easy and beautiful, and you'll be able to swap blooms for easy holiday updates. This tutorial will show you just how simple it is to add a few embellishments to a purchased grapevine or foam wreath base to create a one-of-a-kind door statement. My kind of wreath.

1. Using scissors or pliers (for stubborn wired stems), cut the blooms off of the stems of the flowers.

2. To make sure your wreath looks lively and not too tidy, pull apart the moss slightly to loosen it. After you stretch it apart a bit, place it around the wreath before you begin gluing. You will be able to work much more quickly this way.

3. Plug in your hot glue gun to warm up the glue for a few minutes. Glue in sections, lifting the moss and lightly pressing back down as you work your way around the wreath. Put hot glue on the base of the moss stems and also on the wreath to make sure it adheres. Leave enough space to attach the pretty blooms.

4. Glue the three blooms to the side or center of the wreath.

This wreath can easily be changed from season to season. Pop off the blooms and swap them for different colors, fabric flowers, or ornaments during the holidays. See three more simple wreaths you can create later in this section.

Craft tags, plaques, frames, and boards come in all shapes and sizes at big craft stores. Think outside the box and try this quick project on a multitude of surfaces to keep you more organized.

Chalkboard Tags

Ever wonder why chalkboard surfaces are everywhere these days? Because there isn't an easier, more beautiful, and more useful project to tackle! Labeling your storage not only keeps you more organized, it is pretty, too. Organization you can get excited about is organization you can stick to. True story.

COST: $12
DIFFICULTY: ★
TIME: 30 minutes

You Will Need:

» 4-pack of wooden craft tag
» Paper towels .
» Krylon Chalkboard Spray Paint
» Drill and small drill bit
» Baker's twine or jute

1. Okay, get ready. This is going to be intense. Open the package of craft tags and spread them out on a paper towel.

2. Spray a thin coat of chalkboard paint in a sweeping motion. Let dry for 30 minutes, then spray and dry two more times, for a total of three coats.

3. Using your drill, drill a small hole in the tag.

4. Tie some pretty baker's twine or jute through the tag and use it to label baskets, bins, or boxes throughout your home. Ta-da!

Simple Chalkboard

💲 COST: $10
🔨 DIFFICULTY: ✦
⏱ TIME: 45 minutes

You Will Need:

» **Annie Sloan Chalk Paint in French Linen** (Only Annie Sloan Chalk Paint or colored chalkboard paint will work. Other chalk paints won't create a chalkboard surface.)

» **Nylon paintbrush**

» **Chalk**

» **Decorative tape for framing** (optional)

Oh, The List. I like to refer to our ever-present calendar of to-dos as The List. Life can become overwhelming if we allow our list to get too long, but it can also become overwhelming if we don't have a simple way to keep track of it all. We needed such a list-organizer, yet lacked the space for a full command center. But we quickly realized that you don't need a command center if you have any available flat surface. You can slap some paint on the side of a kitchen cabinet, and voilà! New list maker/wrangler/command center. You can paint a chalkboard on any surface in your home—just pick a wall or a frame or the side of a cabinet. I hope this helps you wrangle your own list!

1. Wipe the surface down if it is really dirty or greasy.

2. Paint three thin coats of Annie Sloan Chalk Paint, allowing full dry time (approximately 30 minutes) between coats.

3. Let the paint set overnight.

4. Season the chalkboard by rubbing the side of a piece of chalk completely over the paint. Wipe off excess dust.

5. If you like the idea of a finished edge, you can paint a frame along taped lines for a sharper edge, or outline the chalkboard with decorative tape. Or if you love a free-handed edge like ours, leave it simply as is. Relieve your brain of your list!

Bottled water
Milk
eggs

You can always trace a pattern or some chalk art onto your new chalkboard when it isn't in list mode. If you'd like, we also have some free printables and patterns for you to download on our site at *www.perfectlyimperfectblog.com/the50homemakeover*!

Painted Apple Baskets

We all know the deal with pretty storage: The bill can add up quickly, especially when we're talking about twenty bins or baskets. Luckily, large craft stores are perfect for finding affordable storage. There are baskets, bins, crates, and more, all waiting to be painted in the color of your choice. You can find all shapes and sizes, just like these mini apple baskets. They are so inexpensive, and stylish once painted. The possibilities are endless—browse that basket aisle with a new set of eyes!

COST: $8
DIFFICULTY: ★
TIME: 1 hour

You Will Need:

» Paper or paper towels for work surface
» 2 apple baskets
» Acrylic paint, any two colors
» Craft paintbrush

1. Spread out your paper or paper towels to create a paint-friendly work surface.

2. Start by painting the body of the basket. You don't have to be very particular when using acrylics—they're very forgiving and create such a beautiful finish, usually in one coat.

3. As the first color dries, you can begin painting the trim in a different color. Let dry before using.

STYLE FILE

There's really no need to paint the inside of your baskets unless you love that look. If so, go for it!

Stenciled Pillow Cover

COST: $20
DIFFICULTY: ★
TIME: 30 minutes

You Will Need:

» **White canvas pillow cover** (can be found at IKEA)

» **Martha Stewart Crafts Fabric Medium**

» **Acrylic or latex paint** (This project uses Pantone Universe for Lowe's in Emerald latex paint.)

» **Measuring spoons**

» **Stir stick**

» **Stencil** (The one pictured can be found at RoyalDesignStencils.com.)

» **FrogTape or artist tape**

» **Small stencil brush**

» **Folded paper towels**

» **Small outlining brush** (optional)

Stenciling sounds like something our grandmothers would do. For a while, patterns and sizes were limited; now, however, stencils come in all shapes, patterns, and sizes. You can find stencils for entire walls, furniture stencils, and small pattern stencils like this whimsical bird. There are patterns out there that are chic and mimic beautiful wallpaper, but are a much more affordable option. Stencils open the door for all kinds of projects—paint patterns on your curtains, tea towels, pillow covers, anything!

1. Wash and dry your pillow cover to remove any sizing (manufacturer's fabric treatment). Iron it if you'd like—or if you're me, throw it in the dryer long enough that it loses some wrinkles.

2. Measure 1 teaspoon fabric medium to 1 teaspoon paint, and mix together with a small stir stick. The paint will be thin, but not runny.

3. Place your stencil on the pillow cover, and tape along the top and bottom edges to hold it in place.

4. Barely dip your brush in the paint, but evenly cover the brush's entire round flat surface. Then, using a circular motion, offload extra paint onto a folded paper towel.

5. Starting on the plastic part of the stencil, swirl your stencil brush onto the cut-out areas, painting in a circular motion, not in an up-and-down stippling motion. You can fill in that way, but painting in a circular motion helps avoid too much paint seeping under the stencil. Trust me; this is valuable information I wish I'd had a long time ago.

6. After you've filled in the design, remove the stencil. Peel from the corner, and lift a little at a time to make sure extra paint hasn't seeped underneath.

7. If you feel like your bird needs a little something extra, use a small outlining brush and freehand paint small dashes to look like a wind trail. Simple, but a fun touch. Plus, mixing handpainted lines with the stenciled image embraces an imperfect look, and helps you successfully pull off painted accents like these semi-handmade pillows.

Most of the time, painting two thinner coats is much better when painting fabric. But fabric medium really thins the paint and makes it more easily absorbed, so it can help you get great coverage in one coat.

Chalkboard Wooden Placemats

by Edie Wadsworth of *Life in Grace*

I'm Edie, and I'm a blogger, a homeschooler, a Lutheran, and a self-proclaimed goddess of the domestic arts. You can find my writing and photography at *Life of Grace*.

These wooden chalkboard placemats will add the perfect touch to your table setting. There's no end to the creative ways you can use them, and they're incredibly cheap and easy to make. Just let your hardware store cut the plywood to size for you, paint the placemats, and then let the creativity begin. Write the names of your family or guests on the boards, or write out part of your menu. The kids can entertain themselves for hours, making doodles and art and writing fun notes. Just use a damp cloth to clean them and start all over. Even without using chalk, the black makes a perfect backdrop for even your most elegant table setting, especially when paired with a metallic charger, or even just a simple white plate. They're also perfect for outdoor dining and will last forever.

 COST: $15-$20 for 5
DIFFICULTY: ★
TIME: 1 hour

You Will Need:

- » **1 piece of plywood, cut into 12" × 20" rectangles**
- » **Fine or medium-grit sanding blocks**
- » **1 quart of chalkboard paint**
- » **6" roller brush**
- » **Chalk**

 1. Sand the plywood with fine/medium-grit sanding blocks to remove any splinters or rough spots.

 2. Paint two coats of chalkboard paint, allowing 1 hour of dry time between coats.

3. Let the chalkboard paint cure for 24 hours, then lay the chalk on its side and rub it all over the board to season it. Wipe away the excess chalk with a soft cloth or paper towel, and enjoy the placemats!

STYLE FILE

Don't stop at simple rectangles. If you're a little more ambitious, cut the plywood into any shape with a jigsaw or circular saw. Think leaves for fall, and ornaments for Christmas.

Pleated Paper Wreath

by Emily Jones of *Jones Design Company*

I'm Emily, and I'm a wife and mom, a blogger, a business owner, a teacher, a self-taught graphic designer, and an artist. I write and photograph the blog *Jones Design Company*.

Here's a take on the ever-popular book page wreath with a bit of a twist. This time, we've used a phone book (free!) and delicate pleats. This gives the wreath a decidedly feminine feel, and gives you a whole new look to try!

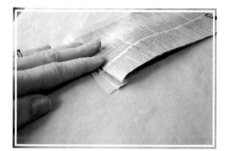

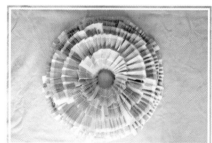

$ COST: $4–5

DIFFICULTY: ★★

TIME: 1 hour

You Will Need:

» Hot glue gun
» Styrofoam wreath form
» Long strip (approximately 3 feet) of cotton or canvas fabric
» Hot glue sticks
» Phone book
» Grosgrain or burlap ribbon for hanging loop, cut to desired length

1. Warm up your hot glue gun. When it's ready, wrap the wreath form in your strip of fabric, adhering the ends with hot glue. This will give you a surface to which to attach the pleated pages.

2. Tear out a stack of pages from the phone book. You can use a full sheet, or tear each in half vertically for a smaller wreath.

3. Starting at one end, fold small pleats into the page and crease to hold. You can stack six to eight sheets and fold them together all at once, to save time.

4. Hold one pleated paper in place against the wreath form and fold up a small portion of the bottom (about ½").

5. Glue pleat to the outside edge of the wreath form. Continue around the wreath, slightly overlapping each pleat to cover the wreath's surface.

6. Continue adding the pleats in layers.

7. Glue a loop of ribbon to the back of the wreath as a hanger.

HANDY HOW-TO

You may want to tear your pages into even smaller pieces as you move towards the center of your wreath. That way, the pleats will not completely cover each other.

Moss Table Runner

This moss table runner is so simple and lovely. Bringing in the outdoors is one way to make your tablescape come alive. Think of this moss table runner as the perfect prop for your next gathering, and an inexpensive way to create a ton of pizzazz. You can create it for a simple spring party, but this idea could translate to any season.

COST: $10
DIFFICULTY: ★
TIME: 20 minutes

You Will Need:

» 3 small bags of craft moss, mixed styles
» Hot glue gun
» Hot glue sticks
» Wood scrap or a board cut to 1' long

1. Make sure to buy a couple of different varieties of craft moss. Some look more artificial and curly, and others look more earthy. Mixing your moss makes the runner look less, well, fake.

2. Pull apart your moss to make it messier and less perfect. You want it to look a little wild.

3. Warm up your hot glue gun. When it's ready, starting at one end and working in sections, place glue all over the board. Be sure to apply glue all the way to the edge so your moss will overhang a bit and hide the wooden board. Place on your table!

STYLE FILE

This runner could be made a million ways. Use leaves and bark to create a centerpiece in the fall, or use artificial snow in the winter . . . the possibilities are endless.

Faux Stitch Napkins

💲 **COST:** $10

🔨 **DIFFICULTY:** ★

🕐 **TIME:** 15 minutes per napkin

You Will Need:

» **4 white cloth napkins**
» **Fabric puff paint**
» **Stencil** (optional)
» **Iron**

Stitching is back again. You'll find it filling the catalog pages of Anthropologie, West Elm, Pottery Barn, and other decor giants. Stitched napkins, quilts, and spreads mimic those passed down by grandmothers, and celebrate the meaning behind the item. This project is made with fabric puff paint (yes, I know!) and inexpensive cloth napkins. You can even use a stencil to make the handmade look as simply as possible!

1. Begin by washing and pressing your napkins to remove any sizing (manufacturer's fabric treatment) that would prevent paint from sticking.

2. Lay your napkin flat, and choose your stitched design. You could freehand straight intersecting lines, or you could use a stencil to create more intricate patterns. Hold your stencil in place with one hand (or tape it down, if you prefer).

3. While holding your stencil firmly, squeeze the bottle of fabric paint to draw small stitch lines within the pattern of the stencil.

4. Let your design dry. Press with an iron to set (or follow the instructions on the back of the paint bottle).

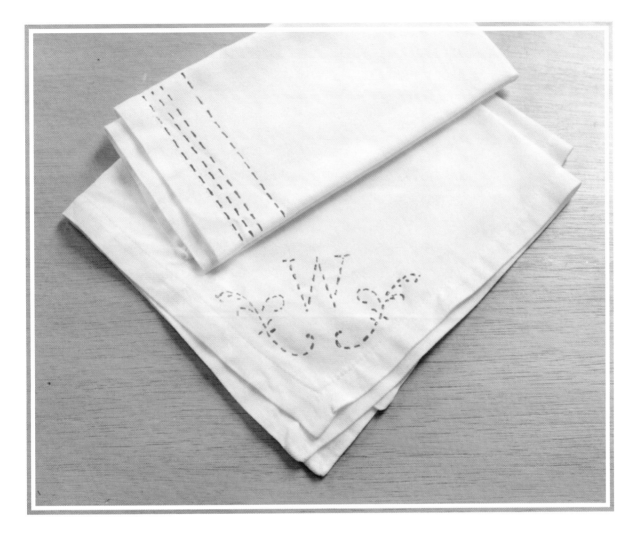

As you squeeze a small amount out of the bottle's fine tip, press the tip into the napkin. When you are finished with that line, press the tip down into the napkin again, then lift up to avoid any paint dripping.

STYLE FILE

This is great as a fall garland, but you can use it for parties, too. Spray it with glitter or artificial snow for a Christmas decoration, or you can always create it with white filters for a wintery or less-rustic look.

Coffee Filter Garland

As the holidays and seasons change, I usually stick to my main decor with a few simple festive additions. I shop discount stores and use 50 percent–off coupons, but sometimes, I like to make just a few decorations myself. I made a coffee filter garland for my daughter's first birthday party, and it was a completely different design. These little coffee filter garland beauties are versatile and perfect for crafting. If you are like me, you probably don't want to spend six hours crafting and making decorations when you could be spending time with your family. This garland is for you, then!

COST: $5
DIFFICULTY: ★
TIME: 30 minutes

You Will Need:

» Baker's twine
» 2 nails or pushpins
» Unbleached cone-shaped coffee filters
» Hole punch

1. Cut the twine as long as you would like the garland to be. Tie one end to a nail. It's easier to see how many filters you need to make the garland full if the twine is stretched out.

2. Work with one coffee filter at a time. Pinch and twist the cone end of the coffee filter while shaping the inside with your hand to create a flower shape. (See the video on our blog at *www.perfectlyimperfectblog.com/the50homemakeover.*)

3. Once you have made your "flowers," punch a hole at the cone end of the filter and string it along the twine.

4. Repeat until your garland is full and fluffy. Twist the filters all the way around the twine so that the garland is full on all sides. This also keeps the filters from sliding around once you are finished, and gives you a chance to shape the garland the way you like.

Wood Slice Wreath

COST: $15
DIFFICULTY: ★★
TIME: 1 hour

You Will Need:

» **Wood slices** (You can buy these at a craft store or online, or you can cut them yourself from a fallen branch in the yard.)

» **Grapevine wreath**

» **Hot glue gun**

» **High-temperature glue sticks** (You will need high-temperature glue sticks if you plan to hang the wreath outside. The low-temperature glue will melt in direct heat.)

» **Wreath door hanger or ribbon**

It's always great to have a few semi-handmade wreaths ready to go for when you want to switch up your seasonal decor. This simple Wood Slice Wreath is striking, full of texture, and looks stunning hanging on your front door or inside your home. Hang it with gold or cranberry satin ribbon to add some color, or use burlap ribbon to keep it neutral.

 1. Place your wood slices around the wreath; layer them and let them overlap.

 2. Warm up your hot glue gun. Once you have chosen the placement of the wood slices, turn them over one at a time, and attach them with hot glue to the wreath.

3. Press firmly to help the glue set. Let the wreath dry for 24 hours before hanging with a door hanger or a ribbon.

STYLE FILE

To add more interest to your wreath, tuck some peacock feathers, book pages cut into leaves, or short cotton stems into one corner.

Handmade Peppermint Wreath

Every year that we celebrate the Christmas season, our traditions grow. The moments shared in the month of December are some of our sweetest. We all have our traditions, our ways of sharing the season with our families. You probably have quite a list of your own. Making this peppermint wreath is a new tradition for our family, and I hope you, too, will make it a tradition in the holiday seasons to come.

COST: $7
DIFFICULTY: ★
TIME: 1 hour

You Will Need:

- » **Peppermints, unwrapped**
- » **White Styrofoam wreath form**
- » **Hot glue gun**
- » **High-temperature glue sticks** (You will need high-temperature heat glue sticks if you plan to hang the wreath outside. The low-temperature glue will melt in direct heat.)
- » **Ribbon or door hanger**

1. Unwrap all of your peppermints, preferably while watching your favorite show.

2. Start anywhere on the inside of the wreath. Place a dab of hot glue on one side of each peppermint and press it onto the wreath form. Work your way around the wreath.

3. Once you get to the second row, stagger the peppermints a bit to cover more of the white of the wreath form.

4. Repeat until the entire wreath is covered in peppermints. Keep the back empty so it can lay flat against a wall or your door. Hang with ribbon or on a door hanger.

STYLE FILE

If you use a door hanger, attach a pretty ornament to the front of the hanger with a dab of hot glue. This will cover the hanger and add some more personality to your peppermint wreath.

Kid Wall Art Gallery

Working the way we do (which is to say, not much of a nine-to-five day), my husband and I try to be purposeful about the time we spend with the little ones. We work quite a lot, so it has become pretty important to us to include our kids in the work we do, and spend focused and purposeful time with them creating. We know you are the same way . . . you have to *make* time for your family in your fast-paced life. This wall canvas project is *so* simple, and it gives you a chance to structure the project a little and then let your own children create art the entire family can appreciate!

You Will Need:

» FrogTape
» Canvas(es)
» Watercolor paints
» Craft paintbrushes
» Cup of water to wash brushes and thin paint

1. While your yahoos are running around, begin taping off your canvas. Feel free to play a little. These aren't going to be perfect, and that's just fine. Use the FrogTape to create patterns, or place it randomly.

2. Choose two or three colors for your kids to use. Blues and greens and a hint of coral or gold are a great starting point.

3. Now, fight every urge you have to hover, and let them paint! Be encouraging, and let them create whatever they'd like.

4. If anything, gently encourage them to add more water in places where the paint goops up. Adding more water here and there will create a beautiful washed pattern.

5. Let your canvas dry. Remove tape gently, and hang the art on the wall!

STYLE FILE

For major impact you and your little ones can be proud of, let them continually add to their body of work, creating a gallery wall as time passes.

Dyed Fabric Napkins

One of the simplest ways to infuse color and personality into your home is with fabrics. Throw pillows take your Plain Jane sofa to spectacular in no time, and patterned curtains dress up your windows in minutes. But sometimes fabric can be expensive, which makes swapping out throw pillows on a whim a little less realistic. Traditional fabric dyes create a highly saturated pigment, but dyeing with Annie Sloan Chalk Paint can give you a more subtle effect. And really, it's as simple as stirring water. This tutorial helps you transform basic neutrals to any color of the rainbow, while giving you more bang for your buck by using one product for many projects. Try it on affordable cotton napkins, curtains, and pillow covers.

COST: $14
DIFFICULTY: ★★
TIME: 30–60 minutes

You Will Need:

» 6 white cotton napkins
» 2 tablespoons Annie Sloan Chalk Paint in Florence
» Large plastic bowl of water
» Measuring spoons

1. Begin by washing your napkins to remove any sizing (manufacturer's fabric treatment) that might prevent the napkins from accepting the color evenly.

2. Mix 2 tablespoons of Florence with approximately ½ gallon of water. You don't have to be exact with this measurement. If you want more color, add more paint one tablespoon at a time. Stir with a spoon until the paint mixes evenly with the water.

3. Place the napkin into the mixture and stir it around until the mixture covers it evenly.

4. Leave the napkin to soak in the tinted water, stirring occasionally to prevent any paint from separating and "tie-dyeing" the finished product. The napkin shown soaked for twenty-five minutes.

5. Leave the napkin in until desired color saturation is achieved. Wring out excess, throw in the washer for a rinse cycle, and dry it on high. The paint will fade, but the wash of color remains. You can always mix in some fabric medium if you would like a more saturated dyed napkin.

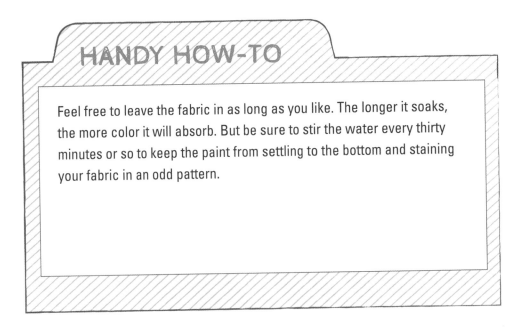

HANDY HOW-TO

Feel free to leave the fabric in as long as you like. The longer it soaks, the more color it will absorb. But be sure to stir the water every thirty minutes or so to keep the paint from settling to the bottom and staining your fabric in an odd pattern.

Twine-Wrapped Bottle

When decorating your home, it's sometimes easy to change a wall color or paint a piece of furniture. But you, like so many, might get stuck once the big changes are in place. How do you decorate your coffee table? Style your bookshelves? Think of accessorizing as the finishing touch on the style of your home. This twine-wrapped bottle is a simple project, and could be replicated in numerous ways with various textures. Simply wrap an old wine bottle in twine, jute, hemp, ribbon, yarn, or even decorative tape.

💰 **COST:** $5
⏲ **DIFFICULTY:** ★
⏱ **TIME:** 30 minutes

You Will Need:

» Old bottle, label removed
» Hot glue gun
» Glue sticks
» Hemp or jute twine

1. If your bottle still has a label attached, soak it in warm water for ten to thirty minutes to remove label. Remove label and dry bottle.

2. Plug in the glue gun and allow to heat up for a few minutes.

3. Place a dab of hot glue in the center of the top of the back of the bottle, about 1" down from the neck. Place one end of your twine in the hot glue and let set for five minutes.

4. Hold the starter piece of twine in place while you wrap the twine tightly around and around the bottle, leaving no gaps in between.

5. Wrap twine all the way to the bottom of the bottle, leaving just enough room so the bottle can still stand. Snip your twine off so that it ends on the back of the bottle. Place one more dab of hot glue at your stopping point. Attach the twine and let set for a few minutes. Style your bottle with a layered vignette on a tabletop or bookshelf.

STYLE FILE

When styling tabletops and shelves, remember this: A flat table is a boring table. Vary the heights of accessories, place your bottle on a stack of books, or even prop a piece of art behind it. I don't follow set rules when styling our home, but using odd groupings is usually visually appealing to everyone. Think three objects nestled together on a bookshelf, three piles of books, or three layered pieces of art.

CHAPTER 3

Upcycling

Inspiration and ideas are everywhere. A side effect of feeling freedom in your decor choices is realizing how many materials around you actually work in the home. I remember the first time I brought home a chicken feeder to use as a small floral centerpiece on a farmhouse table. Cue the shocked husband. It takes some practice to look at everything with an unbiased eye, and to view items with a "it could be this color" lens. Once you get the hang of it, though, you'll be addicted. Oh, and your family and friends? They'll get used to it.

In this chapter, you'll see industrial spools turned into tables, fences turned into wall art, and vintage books turned into a lamp. Go ahead: Open your eyes, look around, and see what you can repurpose into the next best thing.

Spool Side Table

Ah, the industrial spool. They're already table-like, they come in several sizes, and for the most part, they're free. Keep an eye out at your local electrical company and ask if they ever toss leftovers. You'll eventually land a free one—or twelve.

COST: $20
DIFFICULTY: ★
TIME: 30 minutes

1. After hauling your free spool home, you'll want to give it a good sanding to smooth all the rough edges and loose pieces. Using an orbital sander (or sanding blocks), start by sanding with coarse sandpaper.

2. Switch to fine sandpaper next to smooth out the finish.

3. Using the drill and the screwdriver bit, screw each caster into the base of your spool. Three is enough, if they are spaced apart equally.

4. Decorate your new table to your heart's desire.

You Will Need:

» Industrial spool
» Orbital sander.
» Coarse and fine sandpaper pads, or sanding blocks
» Drill and screwdriver bit
» 3 casters
» 12 screws

HANDY HOW-TO

You can always seal your table with polyurethane, but the one pictured was left alone. Feel free to slap a coat of paint on your spool, too!

Scrap Wood Word Wall Art

COST: $4
DIFFICULTY: ★
TIME: 30 minutes

You Will Need:

» **Scrap wood pieces** (approximately 12" wide × 18" long)
» **Sanding block**
» **Acrylic/craft paint** (colors of your choice)
» **Craft paintbrush**
» **Mod Podge**
» **Foam brush**
» **Decorative paper**
» **Stencils**
» **Picture-hanging kit**

Words mean quite a lot to me. I surround myself with them all day: writing, reading, blogging, journaling . . . I'm a word nut. I believe words heal, inspire, move. So when we put together a playroom for our kids, we set out to create a space that inspired them to create and explore the world. Hence, the simplest word art tutorial ever. You can use this idea exactly, or choose words that inspire your own family. Feel free to play with color and patterns to create one-of-a-kind art.

 1. Buff your piece of scrap wood with a sanding block, if needed. Wipe down.

 2. Paint the wood in your shade of choice.

3. After the paint is totally dry, spread on a thin layer of Mod Podge with a foam brush. Cut the decorative paper to be the same size as your board and place it over the Mod Podge. Let dry.

 4. Use stencils and the acrylic or craft paint to create your inspiring words.

 5. After the paint dries, paint on a topcoat of Mod Podge to seal in your work. Let dry.

 6. Attach a picture-hanging kit, and voilà! Hang on the wall and enjoy.

SOAR FLY SAIL

BELIEVE

WISH

{ DREAM BIG }

WHERE TO FIND IT

Have fun with your papers! Layer them for a patchwork look, or spread them out for a cleaner feel. Have fun with color, and don't be afraid to mix pattern choices. My favorite spots for fun paper are Hobby Lobby, Paper Source, and our online shop, Perfectly Imperfect (shameless plug, sorry!).

Reclaimed Wood Wall Art

There is nothing more special than beautifully colored, aged wood. If you're looking for a big impact art piece, this is an easy way to go. You can create inexpensive and super-simple wall art using scrap wood you have lying around.

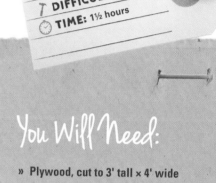

💲 **COST:** $25

📐 **DIFFICULTY:** ★★

⏱️ **TIME:** 1½ hours

1. Have your piece of plywood cut to size at your local home improvement store, and pick up scrap pieces there if you don't have any lying around at home.

You Will Need:

» Plywood, cut to 3' tall × 4' wide

» Scrap wood pieces

» 3 to 5 colors of any kind of paint in 4-ounce sample pots

» Paintbrush

» Wood glue

» Clamps or heavy items

» Picture-hanging kit and wire

2. Lay out your scrap pieces on the plywood first. Be random about it and vary widths and lengths of the wood.

3. After placing all of your pieces, pick them up and add a thick coat of paint to them one by one, varying colors. Painting this way will save you cutting paint in around a million edges. Let dry.

4. Once the paint is dry, grab your wood glue and flip the pieces over. Put a dab of glue in the center and a little along edges, but try not to overdo. The glue will seep out from the edges if you use too much.

5. Turn pieces back over and use wood clamps to set the glue. Or you can be fancy like us, and pile encyclopedias on top.

6. Fasten the picture-hanging hardware to the back of the board, and hang your art! To firmly hang the art, secure it to wall studs using wood screws. You can find the wall studs using a stud finder or by knocking on the wall with the back of your hand. The wall will sound hollow where there is no stud.

Paper-Covered Vintage Books

💲 **COST:** $15

🔨 **DIFFICULTY:** ★

🕐 **TIME:** 1 hour

You Will Need:

» **Old, inexpensive book** (Hardbacks work best, but you can use softcovers, too.)

» **12" × 12" scrapbook paper** (to cover a hardback)

» **X-ACTO knife or scissors**

» **Scotch tape** (Go for the good stuff—it's got to hold well.)

I love vintage books. They're an easy and inexpensive way to infuse personality into a well-styled bookshelf. Having a stash of vintage titles is wonderful, but not all books will look excellent or organized in every space. Unifying your book covers can really identify your style and create major visual impact for little money. Luckily, covering them couldn't be any easier, and it's less than permanent if you're a bibliophile like me.

 1. Lay your book on top of one sheet of paper, lining up the corners of the paper with the back cover of the book.

 2. Fold the other half of the paper over the cover of your book. Keep in mind that the paper won't totally cover the book—we'll fix that in a minute.

3. Keeping the paper wrapped tightly around the book, stand it upright so that the excess paper is coming off the top.

HANDY HOW-TO

If you want the book completely covered, trim another piece of paper and apply to the back of your book. You can skip this step if your books are stacked upright or laying face-up. If the tape isn't holding (which can happen on cloth-covered books), use a small amount of tacky putty instead.

 4. Making sure your paper is in the correct position, make a crease in your paper at the overhang.

 5. Now line up your crease with the blade of the cutting tool, and trim the paper to size.

6. Start covering the front of the book first. Use Scotch tape to attach the paper to the right side of the front cover first. Work your way around the book, pulling the paper tightly as you go and holding the book as straight as possible. Attach the paper with tape. You can either use double-sided tape or use regular tape by rolling it up to create your own double-sided tape. Continue wrapping paper around the book, attaching it with tape.

7. After covering the entire front cover and spine of the book, run something along the spine to create a crease so the paper will hug the book. A rounded end of a craft paintbrush works well, but you can use anything.

Reclaimed Wood Fence Art

by Karianne Wood of *Thistlewood Farms*

I'm Karianne, and I'm the writer, designer, and photographer behind *Thistlewood Farms. Thistlewood Farms* is so much more than the story of a farmhouse. It's about family and tortoises and burlap and shutters and twirly whirly skirts and pancakes and Lee Press-On-Nails and little pieces of paper. It's the story of our dream.

There's just something about reclaimed wood that gives even the simplest of projects character and personality. You can use reclaimed wood from old barns or fences or storage crates. And if you don't have any of those sources readily available, your local home improvement store's fencing department usually has some great resources. Head for the single plank fencing and look for a few pieces that have a little extra weathering. That and about 30 minutes are all you need to create your own reclaimed art piece.

You Will Need:

- » 7 to 10 strips of reclaimed wood, 2-4" x 36"
- » Hand saw
- » Nails or 1" wood screws
- » Hot glue gun
- » Hot glue sticks

1. Cut a fence plank (or board) into a small rectangle 2½" wide by 4" long. Mark a point in the center of the top of the rectangle. From that point, make two diagonal cuts to the lower corners with a hand saw to form the "roof" of the house. Repeat this step to make 9 additional houses.

2. Cut another strip of fence to be 36" long and 2½" wide. Repeat to make seven additional strips. Cut two 14" boards to brace the back. Lay the seven fence planks face-down to create a wood rectangle. Use the smaller boards to attach all pieces together. Place the two 14" boards 3" in from each side and attach to each plank using nails or wood screws.

3. Flip the board over so the front shows and place the houses approximately 3" apart in three rows. Attach the houses with hot glue. Prop the piece on a mantel or a dresser. This casual piece is perfect for layering with fresh cut flowers and smaller art prints.

STYLE FILE

Natural wood pieces look absolutely gorgeous paired with other elements from the outdoors like greenery and pops of crisp white flowers. Sometimes less can be so much more!

Aged Book Bundles

A beautiful space is filled with books. We believe a well-read home is vital to good conversation, racing imaginations, big dreams, and inspiration, but let's be honest: Pretty books look great stacked on a coffee table. Stacking and leaning different titles is just another way you can add texture and interest to your shelves and flat surfaces. In fact, my mama always said a flat table is a boring table. You could buy vintage-inspired book bundles from your favorite retailer, or you could just make them yourself. Plop those guys on any lackluster surface for instant interest and character.

$ COST: $5–10
DIFFICULTY: ★
TIME: 10 minutes

You Will Need:

» **Old hardback books**
» **Fabric scrap** (canvas or burlap works great) or twill ribbon

1. Grab the book near the spine and rip the cover off. Yep, that's it.

2. Tie a grouping of three or four glued insides of the books together with a scrap of burlap, twine, or ribbon.

WHERE TO FIND IT

Check thrift stores for old books. That's where you'll find them for ten to fifty cents each!

Gold Leaf Botanical Prints

You Will Need:

» Pressed leaves
» Sheet of paper
» Small craft paintbrush with soft bristles
» Martha Stewart Crafts Brass Liquid Gilding
» Homestead House Acrylic Paint in eggshell finish
» Burlap or other natural-toned fabric
» Spray adhesive or double-sided tape

Painting pressed botanicals with liquid brass leaf dresses these prints up and brings a bit of femininity to them without going over the top. If you don't run across framed prints, you can easily gather your own leaves and press them between two heavy books. Look for leaves that are wide and thick; dried maple leaves work well.

1. Take the leaves out of the frame and place them on a sheet of paper or board to paint. These will be delicate; handle them gently and keep all children far, far away. I'm pretty sure my two looked at these leaves and they all but disintegrated.

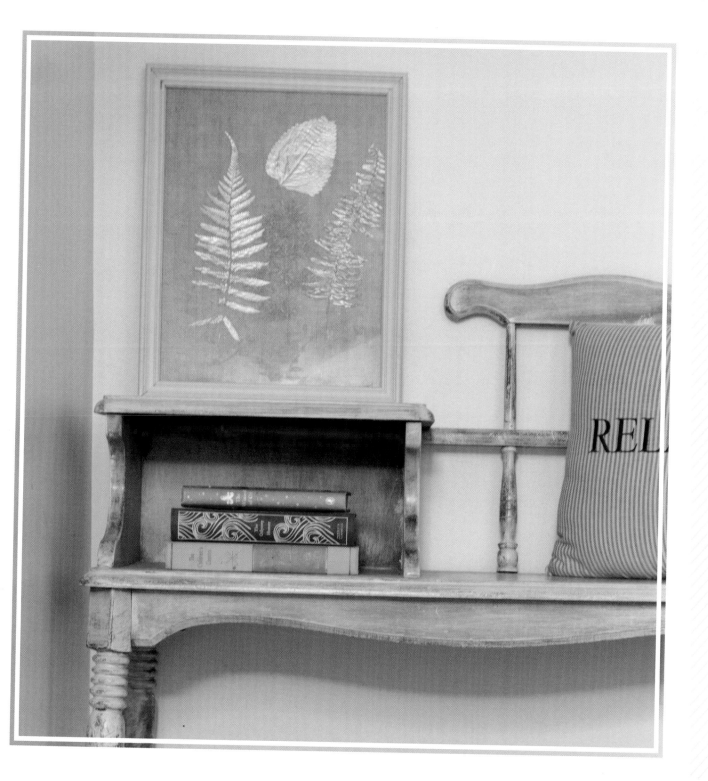

2. Using a small craft paintbrush, dip into the liquid gilding. This is a time when excess paint is a good idea. Your leaves will be too delicate for a lot of drag as you paint. Dab on or gently spread the leaf rather than dragging your brush to apply the paint. Let dry overnight.

3. Paint your frames with the acrylic. This pale blue-grey creates contrast between the frame and the burlap. Acrylic paint adheres really well, so just dip your brush in and go. This paint also doesn't require a topcoat and dries with an eggshell satin sheen. Beautiful!

4. Cut the burlap to the size of the frame's cardboard backing. Using spray adhesive or double-sided tape, attach the burlap to the backing. (You may want to iron your fabric first if it is very wrinkled.)

5. Lay the leaves on the burlap-covered backing, arranging them as you please. Use spray adhesive if they don't stick well to the rough surface of the burlap.

6. Gently lower the frame over the backing and leaves. Fasten the backing to the frame.

HANDY HOW-TO

This project only works with loose paints like the liquid leaf or spray paint. Don't try to use a thick paint with a lot of body, as it could rip your leaves.

Updated Filing Cabinet

Don't be afraid to dumpster-dive to find great pieces like this. You can also run across all kinds of card catalogs, filing cabinets, and other office supply pieces at antique and thrift stores. For small pieces like this cabinet, don't pay too much; you'll find a great deal somewhere. For rare finds like large card catalogs, feel free to splurge a little. With a bit of cleaning or paint, you can create a one-of-a-kind organizational masterpiece for your home.

COST: $10
DIFFICULTY: ★
TIME: 30 minutes

You Will Need:

» Filing cabinet or card catalog
» All purpose cleaner or degreaser
» Acrylic paint, such as Homestead House Acrylic in Early Blue
» Paintbrush

1. If this treasure was found in a trash pile somewhere, or even in a dusty antique store, you may want to give it a good cleaning first. Old wooden pieces like this can acquire a waxy or dusty buildup over time. Use an all-purpose cleaner or a degreaser to remove any gunk left from years sitting unused.

2. Remove any of the pieces you can, like the drawers or filing levels. This will make painting the inside much easier. If they can't be removed, don't worry. Paint as far back as you can reach, and chances are that's as far back as anyone will notice.

3. Paint the whole piece in one coat and let dry. Acrylic paint doesn't require a topcoat, but you can buff with a cloth if needed.

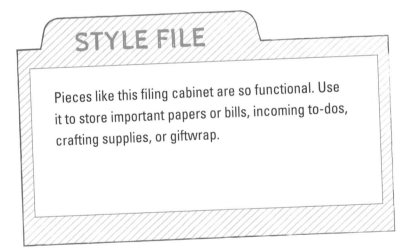

STYLE FILE

Pieces like this filing cabinet are so functional. Use it to store important papers or bills, incoming to-dos, crafting supplies, or giftwrap.

Painted Aged Baskets

COST: $15

DIFFICULTY: ★

TIME: 30 minutes

You Will Need:

» **Acrylic paint** (such as Homestead House in Gallery Blue)
» **Paintbrush**
» **Basket**
» **Soft cloth**
» **Miss Mustard Seed's Antiquing Wax**

Not all baskets are created equal. You've got your Pottery Barn variety, which are perfection. But then, there's the lesser variety—the kind you usually find at a discount or craft store. There is nothing wrong with the shape, but many times, it's the color that's off. Hopefully this project will inspire you to look at almost any item with objective eyes; you just might have a couple of dozen projects already waiting in your home.

 1. Paint a thin (almost dry-brushed) coat of paint onto your basket, avoiding any hardware or leather straps. Let dry and repeat for one or two more coats. You want to create a weathered look, not a thick painted coat.

 2. Once you are satisfied with the paint coverage, apply the antiquing wax. This wax is thin enough to work as a glaze, rubbing on and off to tint your paint and age it slightly.

 3. Allow your wax coat to dry, then put your basket to work!

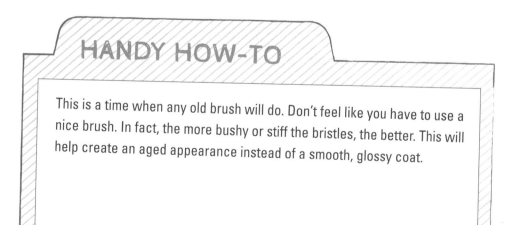

HANDY HOW-TO

This is a time when any old brush will do. Don't feel like you have to use a nice brush. In fact, the more bushy or stiff the bristles, the better. This will help create an aged appearance instead of a smooth, glossy coat.

STYLE FILE

To make your book extra cute (because let's be honest, this project is all about the cute factor), paint the cover a pretty color. You can use acrylic paint, flat latex, chalk paint, or milk paint with a bonding agent.

Vintage Book Catch-All

When we opened our home decor shop in November 2012, there was so much to do and create that our business card display was the *last* thing on my mind. One of our awesome team members and store manager, Natalie, came up with this quick solution. It's such a fun and creative way to store anything paper-related. Use it on your desk, in the kitchen, or anywhere you need to organize important papers.

COST: $0.25–5
DIFFICULTY: ★
TIME: 45 minutes

You Will Need:

» Hardback vintage book

1. Open the book. Starting with the front inside cover page, take the outer edge and fold it in half, toward the spine of the book. Run your fingers along the folded edge to crease it firmly.

2. For the next page, fold the edge away from the previously folded page, toward the center of the book. Crease the fold again.

3. Repeat, alternating the direction in which the pages are folded. This forces the pages to be as tight as possible, and makes the catch-all more full.

4. Arrange with your business cards, recipes, or Christmas cards.

Book Letters

COST: $5
DIFFICULTY: ★
TIME: 30 minutes

You Will Need:

» Pencil
» Font or tracing pattern (optional)
» Old hardback book
» Clamps
» Jigsaw and metal cutting blade

Creating these letters is as simple as tracing and cutting. You could use these letters as bookends, to add style on a tabletop, or hang them on a gallery wall like we did. Cut out initials and give as gifts, or use them in your own home. You could even cut out your house numbers and hang them on the wall, surrounded by an empty frame. The possibilities are endless!

 1. Trace a letter onto your book, then clamp the book to a worktable to hold it steady.

 2. Using your jigsaw and the metal cutting blade, cut along the lines. Make sure you keep the spine intact so that your pages hold together.

 3. You can glue the pages together on the face of each page to keep the letter from opening, but it isn't necessary.

STYLE FILE

Use these letters in a child's room to spell out a name, or use on a mantel or bookshelf to represent the family initial.

do not forget to show hospitality to strangers for in doing so some have entertained angels without knowing

HANDY HOW-TO

Don't be afraid to make holes in your walls. For most projects, you can use Command strips that leave no damage, but for those that require nails like this one, just use smaller picture hangers, and fill the holes with spackle once you move the wall art. For frames and decor 5 pounds and under, use straight pins gently hammered far into the wall. They are surprisingly strong and leave almost no hole.

Vintage Tray Wall Art

This installation of vintage trays and rattan chargers is an inexpensive and creative way to add texture above our buffet in the living room. Notice how striking the combination of color and texture is.

Hunt for trays, plates, or chargers that speak to you. Mix pattern and color; this is not the project for uniformity. You can hang all the trays in a row, but the asymmetry of this arrangement is what makes it so unique.

1. Gather your trays or chargers. Vary the size if you are going with an asymmetrical arrangement.

2. You can always trace the plates onto paper and play with the arrangement on the floor or by hanging the paper cutouts on the wall first. But if you don't have time for such precise tray hanging, just start somewhere and go for it.

3. Continue hanging trays until you reach your desired look. Try hanging wall art at about 60" off the ground, or 6" to 8" above furniture arrangements. It seems to hug the furniture at that height.

COST: $15
DIFFICULTY: ★
TIME: 30 minutes

You Will Need:

» Trays, chargers, or plates
» Plate hangers for standard sizes, or picture-hanging kits for the large sizes

Vintage Art Collection

COST: $14
DIFFICULTY: ★
TIME: 10 minutes

You Will Need:

» Vintage paintings or prints
» Small hammer
» Command strips or small nails

We would all love a home filled with original, meaningful art. While we may not be able to buy original canvases to fill our walls, it's fairly common to run across beautiful vintage or antique paintings. I found all of these paintings at flea markets, each $7 or less. Keep your eyes open for framed paintings. You can always swap the contents and keep the frame to use for future art.

 1. Decide on the position of your paintings. It's best to always hang gallery walls with "the next painting" in mind. Where will it go, and how will the arrangement look then?

 2. Hammer the nails into the wall, or attach the Command strips to the frame. Hang the paintings for your own original art gallery.

STYLE FILE

To unify your collection, paint all of the frames one or two colors. This will tie together completely different subjects.

Suitcases Side Table

Buying a new piece of furniture is not always an option. For those times, think outside of the box. Side tables are the perfect pieces to create. Look around for objects and materials that will stack and arrange to create the piece you need. Stack vintage suitcases for a bedside table like this project, stack crates like the ones in the Crate Storage project in Chapter 4, or even stack a pile of books. Mixing "furniture" like this with storebought styles creates instant personality in your home.

COST: $25
DIFFICULTY: ★
TIME: 15 minutes

You Will Need:

» Three vintage suitcases

1. Wait for it . . . stack the suitcases.

2. All joking aside, stack your suitcases. If the stack leans a little, add some Styrofoam or pieces of scrap wood between the suitcases. You could always attach the suitcases together, but I like the flexibility of using them as a table for now, and moving them elsewhere if needed in the future.

STYLE FILE

Look for flat suitcases so that stacking will be easier. Also, keep an eye out for the striped variety. They'll add a little pizzazz to your vintage "table."

Stacked Book Lamp

COST: $15
DIFFICULTY: ★★
TIME: 30 minutes

You Will Need:

» Stack of vintage books
» Clamps
» Drill
» ⅜" drill bit (or whatever size is required to accommodate the lamp rod)
» Threaded lamp rod
» Lamp kit
» Drum lampshade

Since I love books, I have collected quite a few in the last ten years. Surrounding yourself with collections is a fantastic way to bring your personality and passions into your space. The display of those collections should be well thought out, and tailored to your daily life. You can arrange the things you love by placing them on bookshelves or in a cabinet, but you can also think outside the box. Create a little whimsy and art with the things you love by making this lamp with favorite vintage books.

1. Choose your stack of books. You can glue them together, or leave them loose so you can rearrange them a little differently from time to time.

2. Clamp the books together while you drill a hole in the center of the stack, all the way to the bottom of the books.

3. Drill another small hole from the back in the center of the bottom book.

4. Twist the threaded lamp rod into the books until set.

5. Starting at the back of the bottom book, thread the electrical cord from the kit into the hole, and push up into the threaded rod all the way to the top.

6. Finish the lamp by attaching the electrical cord to the lamp kit bulb base. Cover with a drum shade and plug in.

WHERE TO FIND IT

Shop thrift stores and flea markets for beautiful books whose looks speak to you. You can score them for as little as ten cents each!

CHAPTER 4

Simple DIY

Building furniture and accents is a lot like baking. It can be tricky, but if you follow the recipe, it's not so difficult. I was hesitant the first time my husband built me a desk. I'll admit that his corners did not always line up on those first few projects, but he had created something beautiful and lasting for our home and our family. And his corners got better.

In the Simple DIY section, you'll find loads of simple builds and some more tool-focused projects like a Laundry Hamper, X Coffee Table, Crate Storage, and a Removable Plank Wall. If you have never tackled building before, be brave, take your time, and follow the recipe. Oh, and have fun!

Removable Plank Wall

COST: $40
DIFFICULTY: ★★★★
TIME: 1 day

You Will Need:

» **Wood planks or boards cut to size**
(Ours were reclaimed.)

» **Palm sander**

» **80-grit sandpaper**

» **220-grit sandpaper**

» **Speed square or straight-edge ruler**

» **Pencil**

» **Miter saw or circular saw** (You can also
have your boards cut at your local home
improvement store.)

» **Paint** (optional, but we used Annie Sloan
Chalk Paint in Provence, Old White, and
Versailles)

You probably have oddly placed attic or cellar doors that you only use once or twice a year. Covering that door with planks is one sure way to make the most of odd placement or awkward corners. This project is a simple way to add impact and style to any wall without the permanence of boarding up the door.

1. Gather enough boards to fit your wall. If you don't have access to reclaimed wood, you can use 1" × 8", 1" × 10", or 1" × 12" boards purchased from your local home improvement store.

2. Sand the boards with a palm sander, first with the 80-grit sandpaper and then with 220, until smooth to the touch.

3. Prop a board flat against the wall. Measure the height twice, first on the left corner, then on the right corner. Mark with your pencil.

4. Using your speed square or straight edge, draw a line between the two points.

5. Line up the board in your miter or circular saw and cut the board along the line.

183

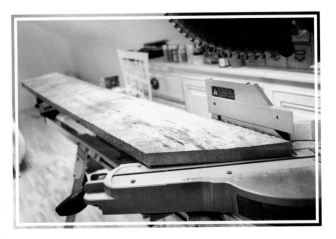

6. Repeat the process with each board and place against the wall. When finished, place a piece of furniture in front of the removable planks to keep them secure.

7. Paint your planks in one or several shades of paint, as you prefer. Painting the boards in several shades creates even more impact on a wall.

HANDY HOW-TO

Since you won't be attaching the boards to the wall, this project is only ideal for a wall tucked behind a large piece of furniture. In our home, our daybed helps secure the boards.

Antique Door Table

Antique doors make my heart flutter. There are a million ways to infuse character into your home, but using salvaged doors, windows, and shutters is one of the easiest ways to do so. They bring an instant story to the spaces they're in. When we found this aqua chippy door, I knew it *had* to become a table. Tables like this are the perfect place to share meals in the summer and relax in the evening.

COST: $35
DIFFICULTY: ★★★★
TIME: 2 hours

Cut List:

» (4) 27-inch 2" × 4½"s (Leg Piece A)
» (4) 27-inch 2" × 4"s (Leg Piece B)
» (2) 19-inch 2" × 4"s (Apron A)
» (2) 76-inch 2" × 4"s (Apron B)
» (2) 27-inch 1" × 2"s, cut at 45-degree angle at each end (Trim Piece)

You Will Need:

» **(3) 2" × 4" × 8' boards** (choose rough or gray boards)
» **(1) 2" × 6" × 10' board**
» **Table saw, miter saw, or circular saw**
» **(20) 3" exterior wood screws**
» **Drill**
» **Kreg Jig** (optional)
» **(8) 2½" Kreg Jig wood screws**
» **(8) 2" wood screws**
» **Clamps**
» **Antique door, or other solid wood door**
» **Spray polyurethane coating**
» **Safety glasses and hearing protection**

1. Cut your boards to size as listed in the Cut List. If you don't own a table or circular saw, many home improvement stores have cutting services available, or may have equipment to rent.

 After your boards are cut in half, attach one Leg Piece A to one Leg Piece B with two 3" exterior wood screws to create an L shape. Do this four times.

3. Drill 2 Kreg Jig (pocket) holes on each end of one side of Apron Piece A.

4. Clamp one Apron Piece A between two of the L-shaped leg pieces, with Leg Piece A laying flat and the attached Leg Piece B pointing into the air. Attach apron to legs with eight 2.5" Kreg wood screws. Repeat for second set of legs.

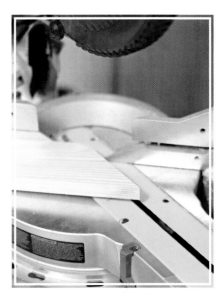

5. Using a circular saw or miter saw, cut 45-degree angles on the ends of each of the 27"-long Trim Pieces. This cut does not have to be exact, but cut as close to the ends as possible.

6. Attach the Trim Pieces with angled ends to the front of the legs with eight 2" wood screws. You'll want them to be 4" from the bottom, and centered between the outside edges of the legs. It's easiest to clamp these to the front of the legs, then flip over to attach from the back.

7. Attach Apron B pieces to the constructed legs using eight 3" exterior wood screws. Attach at a slight angle, from the inside of the leg, lining up the apron flush to the outside of the table leg.

8. Place the antique/solid door on top of the leg frame, centered on each end, and attach from the bottom using four 3" exterior screws on each corner. Screw them in at an angle to prevent the screws from going all the way through the door.

9. To seal the door and prevent any paint from chipping off, spray it with two to three coats of polyurethane. Let dry.

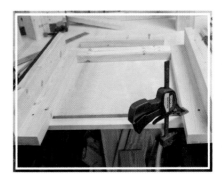

STYLE FILE

Take this project a step further and have a piece of glass cut to size for the tabletop. That will make it fully food safe, and help it handle the weather if it's outside.

Starched Fabric Feature Wall

by Marian Parsons of *Miss Mustard Seed*

I'm Marian, aka Miss Mustard Seed, a wife, mother, lover of all things home, and an accidental entrepreneur, author, freelance writer, and photographer.

I love the look of wallpaper, but it's a long-term commitment. Using starch to apply fabric to a wall is a way to get the look of wallpaper for a lot less money. It can simply be peeled off when a new look is desired, without any damage to the wall. This treatment is not only ideal for those with decorating-commitment phobias, but renters as well!

COST: $47 for starch plus cost of fabric yardage for an 8' × 14' wall

DIFFICULTY: ★★★

TIME: 1 hour, will vary with wall size

You Will Need:

- » **Thick cotton fabric** (Your local fabric or craft store will help you calculate fabric yardage based on the height of your ceilings and width of your wall.)
- » **Scissors**
- » **Measuring tape and pencil**
- » **Level**
- » **Liquid starch**
- » **Paint roller, roller cover, and paint tray**
- » **Tacks**
- » **Gloves** (optional)
- » **X-ACTO knife** (optional)
- » **A second pair of hands is strongly recommended.**

1. Wash your fabric and dry first. Some fabrics come with a border showing manufacturer's instructions or item numbers. Trim that off with scissors.

2. Measure wall width and mark where you'd like to begin the fabric panel. Use a level and pencil to mark a plumb line. Measure the height of your ceiling as well, making note of your measurements. Cut fabric panel to size of wall height.

3. Pour the starch into the paint tray and load the paint roller. Roll the starch onto the wall where first panel will be positioned.

4. Starting from the top, line the edge of the fabric panel up with the plumb line, and place the fabric over wet starch. One of you should apply the fabric, while the other should smooth the fabric down as you apply. Use tacks to temporarily hold the fabric in place. Smooth with hands until fabric is wrinkle-free. Roll over once more with starch.

5. Cut the second panel, making sure the fabric's printed pattern lines up with the previously cut panel. Repeat the previous step with this second panel and all other panels, until the wall is covered. Allow starch to dry, and you're done!

HANDY HOW-TO

Simply peel off the fabric when you're done with the look or it's time to move. You can even wash the fabric and reuse it! To be sure this treatment will be removable in your home, apply a test scrap of fabric in an out-of-the-way area before starching the entire wall.

Simple Map Wallpaper

by Melissa Michaels of *The Inspired Room*

My name is Melissa and I'm the creator of *The Inspired Room*, a decorating blog. I love to share about my own home and things that inspire me about decorating, homemaking, and organization.

You can create a wallpapered map wall with paper and push pins! Heavy-duty wrapping paper or maps from specialty paper stores are the perfect easy solution for a splash of style in any room.

COST: $40 (price will vary with wall size)
DIFFICULTY: ★
TIME: 1–2 hours

1. Start in one corner of your wall. Line the map up with the corner and tack it in place with push pins. Leave the other edge unpinned until you place the next map. Pin the next map, and repeat.

2. Vary the way you hang your map paper. Line some up and leave the entire design showing, and overlap others for a patchwork effect. This will create meaning and depth for the look, and it really celebrates the fun wall treatment.

You Will Need:

» Heavyweight map paper or vintage maps
» Push pins
» X-ACTO knife (optional)

WHERE TO FIND IT

We got our maps from Paper-Source.com, but you could use heavy duty scrapbook paper or even vintage maps you find along the way to create the same look. Use atlas pages to fill in the smaller gaps.

Cork Wall Treatment

You Will Need:

- **Cork panels** (Amcork.com has panels that come in different patterns and colors.)
- **Second set of hands**
- **Level** (optional)
- **Nail gun or Liquid Nails adhesive**

Inspiration is all around us. Really. But sometimes you want to corral that inspiration into one handy spot. An inspiration board to hold fabrics and paint chips and lovely photos is a great way to keep your creative juices flowing. But if you're like me and don't have room for hanging a framed corkboard, you can use stand-alone cork panels to create a board on the back of a door. Plus, using beautifully patterned cork turns this utilitarian tool into art for your home. Use this cork treatment for keeping your family organized, displaying art, or hanging on to frequently used recipes.

1. Unpack your cork and let it sit in the room where you will hang it for about two weeks. This allows the cork to expand and contract depending on the general room temperature and humidity.

2. Have Matt—er, someone who loves you—hold the cork in place. Use a level to keep the cork straight if you're worried about it. If you're hanging your cork on the back of a door, you can just line it up with the side of the door to keep it straight. Attach it to the wall with the nail gun or the Liquid Nails adhesive.

3. Add more cork pieces with the nail gun until you create your desired size and shape.

If you wish to cover an entire door or a specific wall, you can easily trim the cork with an X-ACTO knife.

HELLO

197

X Coffee Table

You Will Need:

» (2) 2" × 4" × 8' boards
» (4) 2" × 2" × 8' boards
» (1) 1" × 12" × 8' boards, trimmed to 11¼" in width
» (5) 2" × 6" × 8' boards
» Drill with countersinking bit
» Pocket hole jig (such as a Kreg Jig)
» 1¼" and 2½" pocket hole screws (100-pack each)
» Measuring tape
» Pencil
» Compound miter saw or circular saw with carpenter's square
» Safety glasses and hearing protection

We love building our own furniture. Matt tends to pull plans out of his own head, but sometimes it is nice to have a plan right in front of you. We love working with Ana White (*www.ana-white.com*), so we asked her to draw up the plans we used for our own coffee table. You'll love how simple and easy to follow her instructions are! If you are nervous about your furniture builds, take a breath, roll up your sleeves, and follow these simple steps to build your own beautiful, solid wood coffee table.

Cut List:

» (4) 16-inch 2" × 4"s (legs)
» (4) 41-inch 2" × 2"s (side trim)
» (4) 22½-inch 2" × 4"s (end trim)
» (2) 41-inch 1" × 12"s (bottom shelf)
» (5) 52-inch 2" × 6"s (tabletop boards)

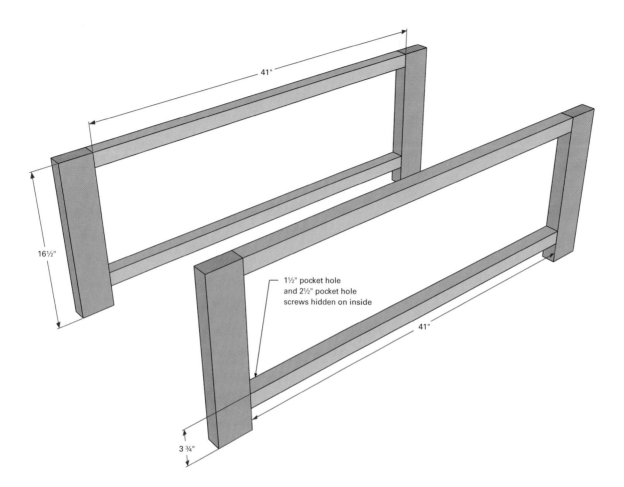

41"

16½"

3 ¾"

41"

1½" pocket hole
and 2½" pocket hole
screws hidden on inside

1. Cut your boards to the diagrammed lengths with the saw. If you don't have a saw, many hardware stores will provide cutting services or tool rentals.

2. Drill a single 1½" pocket hole on each end of the 2" × 2" side trim boards (the 41"-long 2" × 2"s). Using 2½" pocket hole screws, attach the side trim boards to the leg boards (the 16½" long 2" × 4"s), with the top joint flush to the top of the legs. The bottom trim is attached with a 2¼" spacing underneath.

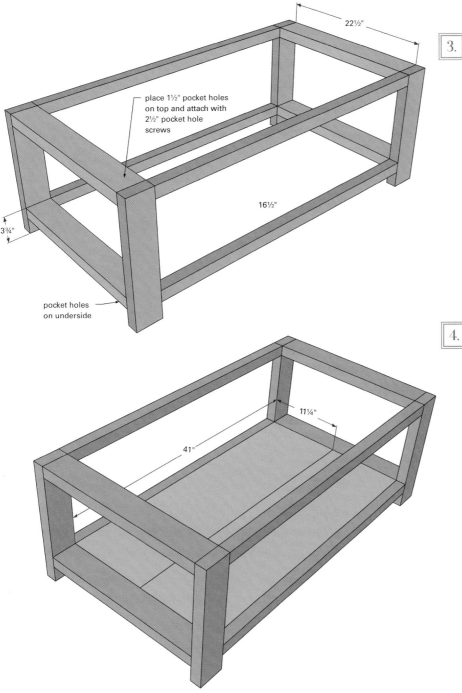

place 1½" pocket holes on top and attach with 2½" pocket hole screws

22½"

16½"

3¾"

pocket holes on underside

11¼"

41"

3. Drill two 1½" pocket holes on each end of each of the end trim boards (the 22½"-long 2" × 4"s). Using 2½" pocket hole screws, attach the end trim boards to the legs, with the top boards flush. Leave 2¼" spacing underneath the bottom trim board.

4. Drill ¾" pocket holes along one long edge of one bottom shelf board (a 41"-long 1" × 12" board), placing pocket holes approximately 8" apart. Use these pocket holes to attach the other bottom shelf board with 1¼" pocket hole screws to create the bottom shelf. Make sure the bottom shelf fits, trimming if needed. Then drill ¾" pocket holes around the outside edges of the bottom shelf on the underside, approximately 8" apart. Attach the bottom shelf with 1¼" pocket hole screws to the side and end trim boards.

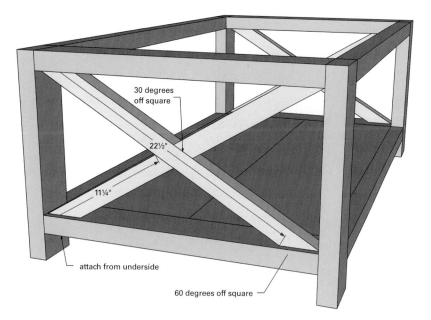

30 degrees
off square

22½"

11¼"

attach from underside

60 degrees off square

5. With the remaining 2" × 2" boards, cut the long X boards; with both ends cut at 60 degrees off square, ends are parallel to each other. If your saw does not cut this angle, you can simply hold an uncut 2" × 2" board in position, mark the angle, and cut along your marks. Attach inside ends, and then repeat these steps with the smaller X boards.

6. Now just the tabletop left! Take four of the tabletop boards (the 52" long 2" × 6" boards) and drill 1½" pocket holes about 8" apart down one edge. Attach the table-top boards together with 2½" pocket hole screws. Place the tabletop face-down (pocket holes upward) and position the base on top, with equal overhangs. Attach the table-top to the side trim and end trim boards with 2½" screws.

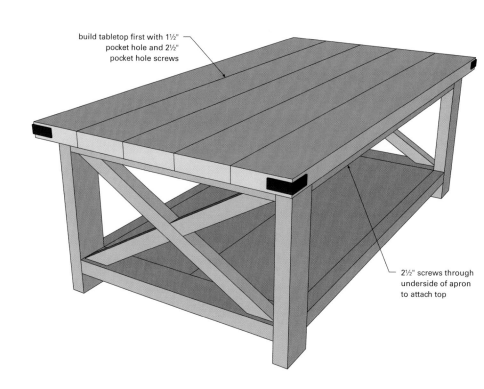

build tabletop first with 1½" pocket hole and 2½" pocket hole screws

2½" screws through underside of apron to attach top

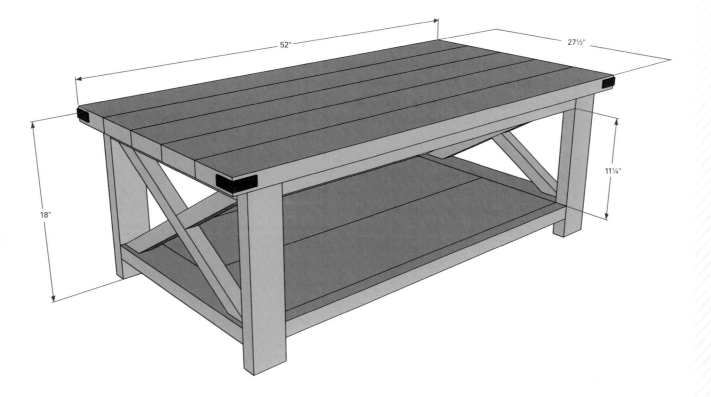

52"

27½"

11¼"

18"

Personalize this coffee table by adding hardware, such as corner brackets, at corners, or even caster wheels. Stain or paint to fit your design taste and space. What to do with the wood scraps? Build a matching end table! You can find those plans at *www.ana-white.com.*

Pallet Wall Clock

Huge wall clocks make such a bold statement, and anytime I spot one in a room, I'm immediately drawn into the space. They can be quite pricey, but you can make your own using clock parts and thin pallet boards. Use this tutorial as a guide to create your own one-of-a-kind repurposed showstopper. You could use pallet wood (like we did), new wood, or even a sheet of bead board.

$ COST: $19
DIFFICULTY: ★
⏱ TIME: 1 hour

1. Pull apart your pallet if it's still in one piece. Remove any nails and lightly sand the pallets if they are very rough to the touch.

2. Cut each board to 36" wide. This clock used ten boards, but it will vary depending on board size. The goal is to have roughly a 3-foot by 3-foot-square clock. Keep in mind this is made from pallets, and a ½" here or there will only add to the character.

You Will Need:

» **Pallet boards**
» **Palm sander** (optional)
» **(40) 1" wood screws**
» **Drill**
» **⅝" drill bit** (or size of your motor attachment)
» **Clock hands and motor** (can be found at Coastal Tide Clocks on eBay)

 3. Lay out the pallet boards to make a square. Arrange the spacing to your taste and vary the coloring of the boards for visual interest.

4. Flip the boards over so the front of the clock is facing down, and attach them with four 1" wood screws to two 3-foot pallet boards running vertically along each side of the square. Two screws should be attached at each end of each vertical support board, for a total of four screws per support board, and offset to keep the boards square.

5. Flip the clock over so that the front is facing up. Measure to find the center, and drill a hole there to hold the clock motor.

6. Attach the clock motor stem and hands according to package instructions. Attach picture hanging hardware to the back of the clock, and attach to the wall using screws.

We left our pallet clock completely natural. It was so architecturally striking that I couldn't paint numbers on it. However, you could paint on numbers, Roman numerals, dots, or slashes. You could also go more industrial and use large iron nails in place of the numbers.

Pallet Wine Rack

💲 **COST:** Free

🔨 **DIFFICULTY:** ★★★

⏱️ **TIME:** 2–3 hours

Building with pallets is all the rage these days, and it's easy to see why. You can find free pallets at many warehouse stores, they're easy to break down, and the wood has a distinctive, reclaimed look to it. This rustic rack includes stem glass storage on the bottom to keep your glassware handy.

You Will Need:

» **Circular saw**

» **Small pallet** (Look for one with a central support board inside—it helps tremendously!)

» **Drill**

» **3½" hole saw bit**

» **Finish-nail gun**

» **1½" finish nails**

» **Miter saw**

209

1. Using the circular saw, cut the pallet on the top and bottom, along one side of each side of the center support board to create 2 smaller rectangles.

2. Brace your pallet by clamping thin boards closely around the area where the hole saw bit will cut the holes for the wine bottles. This will help stabilize the bit and provide a more regular spacing between the holes.

3. If you prefer, trace circles onto the pallet beforehand instead of using the boards/clamp method as a guide for drilling holes.

4. Drill circle openings along the pallet. Try three slots; odd numbers are pleasing to the eye.

5. After drilling all openings, place a wine bottle into one. Mark on the back board where the neck of the bottle should rest. Attach a scrap piece of the pallet to the back board along that mark with either a finish-nail gun or 2" wood screws. You can use different widths and thicknesses for the back brace boards.

6. Measure the width of the wine rack to measure for the back support board. Cut another pallet board.

7. Using the miter saw, make three small notches halfway through the board, about ¼" to ½" wide each. Feel free to start with ¼"; place your stemmed glasses inside and try it out. If it's a little snug, move up to ½".

8. Attach the stem display 1–2" from the bottom of the wine rack. Use two small scrap pieces to lower it (on the back) if needed. Hang the rack by using screws and a picture hanging kit. If your pallet wine rack is heavy, secure it to the studs in the wall using wood screws.

HANDY HOW-TO

If there is a back board where the bottle neck should rest, drill a hole large enough for the bottle to fit.

HANDY HOW-TO

Any time you are screwing boards together, stagger the screws to create more stability.

Hand-Painted Sign

You can't beat a pretty vintage sign. Hanging or propping one in a room brings about instant charm and nostalgia. Hand-painted vintage signs are worth a lot, and depending on the dealer, can be pretty highly priced. And often either the price or the look isn't quite right. But the amount of time it takes to build and paint your own? Little to no time at all. Search online for inspiration, or choose meaningful words and get painting!

COST: $20
DIFFICULTY: ★
TIME: 1½ hours

You Will Need:

» **Table saw**
» **Two 1" × 6" × 12' yellow pine boards**
» **Drill**
» **⅛" wood screws**
» **Paint** (For this look, use Homestead House acrylic in Early Blue, Annie Sloan Chalk Paint in Pure White, and Martha Stewart Basic Crafts Paint in Christmas Red.)
» **Paintbrush**
» **Letter stencils** (optional)
» **Picture hanging kit**
» **25-lb picture hanger**

1. Using a table saw, cut the pine boards into 8 pieces each measuring 32", or have them cut at your local home improvement store.

2. Lay six boards out horizontally and face down. Using a drill and ⅛" wood screws, attach the two remaining boards to the back of the six face-down boards, 2" in from the ends.

3. Turn the sign back over. Paint one coat of the Early Blue acrylic paint. Acrylic paint is high quality, and it usually covers in just one coat.

4. Trace lettering onto your sign, or just freehand it. Vintage signs shouldn't feature perfect fonts, so feel free to play around with it. Start with a pencil outline and then fill in with paint.

5. Outline your letters in a darker or contrasting color to make them stand out a little bit more. Hang your art using a picture hanging kit and a 25-lb picture hanger.

Fabric Frame Keepsake

by Ashley Mills of *The Handmade Home*

Hi, I'm Ashley, and my husband, Jamin, and I began our adventure together as college sweethearts, and now we run the popular home-design website *The Handmade Home.*

This fun fabric frame is a super-easy way to display anything from family photos to one-of-a-kind keepsakes. A larger-than-life version lends itself to personal and meaningful art, such as the envelope from my great grandparents' marriage certificate.

COST: $40–50

DIFFICULTY: ★★★

TIME: 1 hour

You Will Need:

- » 2' × 4' × ½" sheet of MDF
- » Tape measure
- » Pencil
- » Chalk line or straight edge
- » Circular saw
- » Jigsaw
- » Eye and ear protection
- » About 2 yards of fabric of your choice
- » Scissors
- » Hot glue gun
- » Hot glue sticks
- » Painter's tape (optional)

1. On your MDF, mark in 10" from the edge in both directions on all 4 corners. There should be 8 total marks.

2. Take your chalk line or straight edge and draw a line from each top corner mark to each bottom corner mark on two sides. This creates the vertical sides of your frame. Now connect the marks on the top, drawing a straight line from the left to the right. Repeat to create the bottom of your frame. You should now have a frame drawn out on the MDF sheet.

3. Use your circular saw to cut along the lines. Place the guide mark and the blade on the line. Slowly raise the blade, engage the saw, and lower the blade back onto the line, without moving the guide marker from the line. Cut up and down on all four sides, stopping short of the corners. You will have cut a rectangle out of the middle of the MDF, leaving a frame.

4. Use your jigsaw to complete the cut on the corners so the middle falls out of your frame. You should have a completed rectangle frame.

5. Cut the fabric length down to multiple 16" strips. Make a single cut, any width you choose, in one of these 16" sections. Then rip each piece of fabric in two. Continue this process, varying the width of the cut.

6. Tack down one end of a strip of fabric on the back of the MDF with hot glue, then wrap it around the front of the frame. Take the other end of fabric and hot glue to the backside. Wrap the fabric around the MDF frame over and over and glue to the back.

7. Secure your photo to the frame with double-sided painter's tape for easy removal, or use hot glue for a more secure hold.

8. Now hang your frame!

STYLE FILE

Hang this frame with a simple picture hanging kit, or lean it against your fave piece of furniture. Enjoy!

HANDY HOW-TO

If your wood has a lot of grain, use a stain conditioner before staining. It will help the wood accept the stain evenly, leaving no blotching at all.

Herringbone Headboard

It may seem intimidating, but one of the easiest DIY builds you can tackle is a simple headboard. I know it seems a little scary, but truly, it is straightforward and inexpensive. If you're like us, you probably put off spending time and money on your bedroom until you've tackled other rooms. We leave our most personal space until the bitter end. Change that with this farmhouse headboard, which gets extra pizzazz from the mock-herringbone pattern. The result is a fabulous statement headboard you can cherish for years to come. So come on, already. Spend some time on *your* space.

COST: $50
DIFFICULTY: ★★★
TIME: 4–5 hours

You Will Need:

- » (4) 1" × 4" × 12' boards
- » (2) 1" × 6" × 12' boards
- » (1) 1" × 3" × 8' board
- » (1) 4' × 8' sheet of ½" MDF or particle board
- » Table saw or circular saw
- » Wood glue
- » 2" wood screws
- » 1" wood screws
- » Square
- » Fine-grit sandpaper
- » Paint or stain of your choice (The headboard shown uses Rust-Oleum Sunbleached Wood Stain.)

Cut List:

(These measurements are for a queen-size headboard.)

- » (1) 58⅛" × 48" MDF (A)
- » (2) 60-inch 1" × 4"s (cut from 1" × 6") (B)
- » (2) 60-inch 1" × 1⅜"s (cut from 1" × 6") (C)
- » (1) 51⅝-inch 1" × 4" (cut from 1" × 6") (D)
- » (1) 59⅝-inch 1" × 1⅜" (cut from 1" × 6") (E)
- » (2) 51⅝-inch 1 " × 3"s (F)
- » (1) 40½-inch 1" × 3" (G)
- » (1) 59⅝-inch 1" × 1" (H)
- » (1) 63-inch 1" × 6" (I)

1. Cut boards to the measurements in the Cut List. Cut MDF down to size with your table saw. Alternatively, have the cutting done at your home improvement store.

2. To create the headboard legs, attach board (C) to board (B) to form a small L-shape, using wood glue and 2" wood screws. Repeat this step with the other set.

3. Attach the legs to MDF Board (A) from the back, using wood glue and wood screws. Board (C) will be pointing down and covering the side edge of MDF Board (A), and Board (B) will be flush with the top and attached to the front of Board (A).

4. Attach one Board (F) from the back, using wood glue and wood screws. It should be flush to the bottom edge of the headboard between the leg pieces.

5. Attach Board (G) to center of headboard from the back, using wood glue and 1" screws. It should be centered with 29⁵⁄₁₆" on either side.

6. Attach one Board (F) to the headboard leaving 1" between the top of the Board (F) and the headboard, using wood glue and 1" screws from the back. This should make the top of what looks like the letter I on the front of the headboard. Don't worry about the space from the top; it will be covered up later.

7. Start cutting diagonal boards at a 45-degree angle. Begin by cutting the end off of the first board—this will be our corner piece. For the rest of the pieces, the long edge of the first board should be the length of the short edge of the second board. Start in the top left-hand corner of the headboard, with the boards angling toward the bottom middle. The cut angles will be angled away from you when you hold the board. Don't attach these boards yet; just lay them in place to be sure everything will fit together well. Also, you should be able to use these boards as templates for the second side.

8. Continue cutting each board in this manner until you get to the middle corner of the headboard. The board that fits in the corner, when cut like all of the others, should fit on the left, but the tip should stick up in the middle. Use a square or a straight edge to draw a line to trim the board to fit.

9. When the first board reaches the middle, you can use that board as the template to create the next four boards. The angles of these boards will be cut in the same direction.

10. Once you reach the bottom left corner, cut it the same length as the board before, and use the square to draw a line to cut off the excess tip.

11. Now continue cutting the remaining four boards, but this time the angles will be slanted in toward you.

12. Once the first side is complete, you can start over on Step 7, or you can use the boards as templates to make the second side.

13. Once all boards are laid out and fit in place, attach to headboard with glue and with 1" screws from the back.

14. Attach Board (H) to Board (E) using wood glue, aligning the boards so that they are flush with one another at the top.

15. Attach boards from Step 9 to the top of the headboard using 2" wood screws from the back. This will create a nice molding leading up to the top board.

16. Attach Board (I) to the top, perpendicular to the headboard, aligning it to be flush with the back of the headboard. This board will hang over on all sides but the back. Attach using wood glue and 2" wood screws from the top.

17. Lightly sand with fine sandpaper to smooth the surface. Stain if desired. This project uses Rust-Oleum Sunbleached Wood Stain for a light and airy look.

Framed Bathroom Mirror

💰 **COST:** $50
🔨 **DIFFICULTY:** ★★★
⏱ **TIME:** 1½ hours

You Will Need:

» **Thick preprimed molding**
» **Measuring tape**
» **Miter saw**
» **Emerald Enamel paint by Sherwin Williams in Snowbound**
» **Paintbrush**
» **Mirror adhesive or construction glue**
» **Wood glue**
» **Spackle**

You have them. We have them. Simple builder-grade box mirrors. They work wonderfully, but they lack in the personality department. You can quickly and inexpensively add molding to the basic framework to create a gorgeous oversized framed mirror.

1. Measure the height and width of your mirror.

2. Measure a piece of your molding to the same length as the height measurement of your mirror. Cut the ends at a 45-degree angle with a miter saw, then repeat for a second piece of the same length. These will be the side pieces of your frame. Repeat for the two pieces of molding measured to the length of your mirror's width, for the top and bottom of your frame. You can also have your molding strips cut at your local home improvement store.

3. Paint the boards before you attach them. One coat should be enough.

4. Attach the molding with mirror adhesive right along the edge of the mirror. Make sure to line up the corners as you go.

5. Attach the corners together with a little wood glue, wiping away the excess.

6. Spackle any crevices where the moldings line up at the corners to fill in any gap, if necessary.

STYLE FILE

Feel free to choose unique styles of molding and paint it any color you'd like. There are simple moldings, and there are also more ornate French-inspired trim choices. Go with your gut and choose the one you love.

223

Faux Planked Wall

Plain sheetrock walls are a little boring. But over time you can jazz them up by adding more molding, trim, and eventually some wood planked walls. Adding a wood treatment is not always the easiest or cheapest option, so this project takes a different approach. You can find sheets of laminate faux wood paneling in the home improvement store for a fraction of the cost of real wood. I admit, I love a real wood wall when I have it planned and budgeted, but this is a great option to save cost and time. In fact, we used this treatment in our dining room to completely change the look and feel of the room!

| COST: $50 |
| DIFFICULTY: ★★★ |
| TIME: 1–4 hours, depending on wall size |

You Will Need:

- » Measuring tape
- » Table saw
- » 4' × 8' sheets of paneling
- » Finish-nail gun and finish nails
- » Stud finder (optional)
- » Hot glue gun
- » High temperature glue sticks (Adhesion will be better with high-temperature glue sticks.)
- » Foam rollers (one for the primer, one for the latex paint)
- » Oil-based bonding primer
- » Sherwin Williams Emerald Enamel Latex paint in the shade Benjamin Moore's White Diamond

1. Begin by measuring your walls from the bottom of the ceiling trim down to the top of the baseboards.

2. Cut the paneling to be the same height as your walls. You can also have your paneling cut at your local home improvement store.

3. Line up each board on top of the baseboard. These are thin enough to sit on top of the baseboard without having to remove the trim and reattach.

4. Have a friend (or someone you tricked into helping you) hold the paneling sheet onto the wall while you nail the panel to the wall. It's helpful to nail the paneling to the studs in your wall. If not, the weight of your paneling could pull a nail out of the drywall. The nails are more secure when nailed into the stud.

5. Nail the panel into the wall at the bottom, middle, and top in the center of the sheet of paneling, at all four corners, and in the middle of each side. Repeat until all the panels have been hung.

6. If you see the paneling buckle here and there, you can use hot glue to hold it down to the wall. That's right, hot glue. If your sheet is pulling away from the wall, simply wedge the hot glue gun behind the panel where it is buckling, and apply some hot glue to the wall or back of the panel. Press and hold the panel against the wall for a minute or two until set.

7. Using a foam roller, add a coat of primer to the panels and let dry. Then add a coat of the latex paint and let dry. You might need to add another coat of latex paint for more coverage.

HANDY HOW-TO

Oil-based paints and primers can be tricky to work with, but they are perfect for working with laminate or slick surfaces. If you work quickly and use a foam roller to apply the primer, then you will avoid brushstrokes. Buy inexpensive rollers so you can simply toss them when finished.

Laundry Hamper

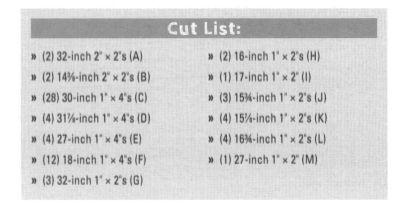

We have slowly been simplifying the way our house works for us, and building this laundry hamper was one way to tackle the laundry beast. And this isn't just any laundry hamper. It is solid pine, sturdy and roomy, with two compartments for sorting laundry as it comes into the space. If you're like us and need help tackling the laundry issue (please tell us we aren't the only ones!), then this hamper is for you!

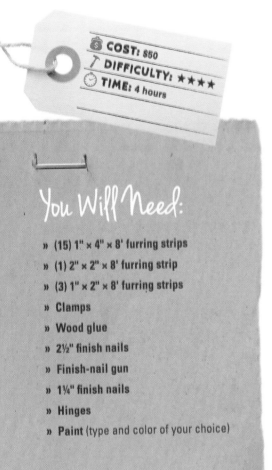

COST: $50

DIFFICULTY: ★★★★

TIME: 4 hours

You Will Need:

» (15) 1" × 4" × 8' furring strips
» (1) 2" × 2" × 8' furring strip
» (3) 1" × 2" × 8' furring strips
» Clamps
» Wood glue
» 2½" finish nails
» Finish-nail gun
» 1¼" finish nails
» Hinges
» Paint (type and color of your choice)

Cut List:

» (2) 32-inch 2" × 2"s (A)
» (2) 14⅜-inch 2" × 2"s (B)
» (28) 30-inch 1" × 4"s (C)
» (4) 31⅛-inch 1" × 4"s (D)
» (4) 27-inch 1" × 4"s (E)
» (12) 18-inch 1" × 4"s (F)
» (3) 32-inch 1" × 2"s (G)
» (2) 16-inch 1" × 2"s (H)
» (1) 17-inch 1" × 2" (I)
» (3) 15¾-inch 1" × 2"s (J)
» (4) 15⅞-inch 1" × 2"s (K)
» (4) 16¾-inch 1" × 2"s (L)
» (1) 27-inch 1" × 2" (M)

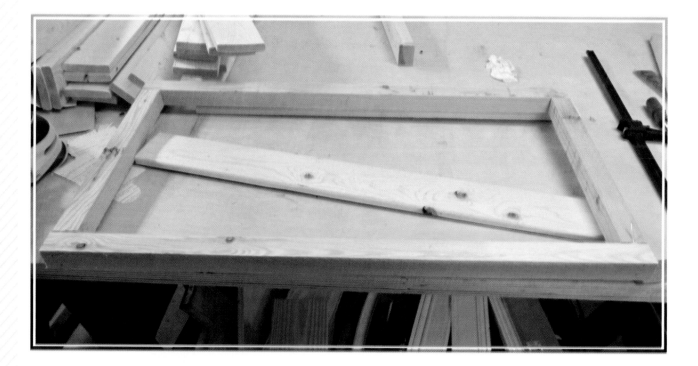

1. Cut the boards on the cut list, or have them cut at your local home improvement store.

2. For the frame of the base, make a rectangle with two (A) 2" × 2"s and two (B) 2" × 2"s. Clamp, and attach them inside the rectangle using wood glue. Place 2½" finish nails in the ends with a nail gun.

3. Now make the slatted bottom of the laundry basket. Attach one (G) board in the center of the frame using 1¼" finish nails. Attach four (D) boards equally spaced to the rectangle frame.

4. Use the (I) board to create the partition base. Nail it 15" from the left side.

5. Attach the (M) board to the middle, perpendicular to board (I), for the center divider.

6. Measure ⅝" in from the side of the rectangle frame to leave room for the top frame. Attach center divider boards (E) on both sides of board (M), equally spaced apart.

7. Now build the front outside wall. Attach nine (C) boards, equally spaced apart, to the base, making sure they are flush on each end. This completes your front.

8. Now build the two sides. Attach five (C) boards to each side of the base, placing them flush on the front with a slight overhang on the back. This completes your sides.

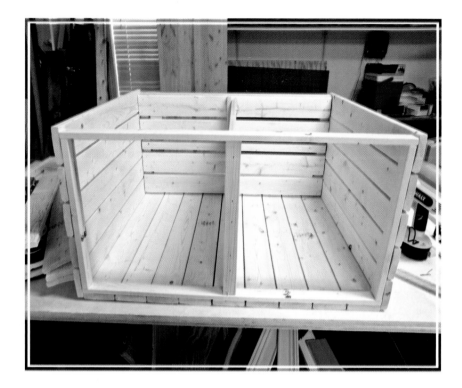

 9. Build a frame for the top. Attach (G) boards horizontally to two (J) boards running vertically. Now attach the frame to the top of the basket. Keep your boards spaced equally apart at the top and bottom while attaching the final frame.

10. Build the back of the basket by attaching nine (C) boards, equally spaced apart.

11. Now attach the center frame board to the center divider boards with 1½" finish nails.

12. Build the lid frames using (K) and (L) boards. Clamp if needed.

13. Attach the frame with the hinge at the back of the laundry basket. Be sure the square lids are close but not touching, and that the back is flush.

14. Cover the top hinged frames by attaching six (F) boards, touching in the center and the back so that the front and sides overhang. Use 1¼" finish nails to attach.

 15. Paint!

HANDY HOW-TO

While this project requires a lot of steps, it is relatively simple to build. By using only furring strips (also called laths or battens) and a finish nailer, we kept the cost and complexity down.

Wood Slat End Table

Sometimes the simplest designs are the most striking. We needed an end table in our living room, but I wanted something with clean lines and a shelf. This slat end table we designed is functional and pretty to boot. You can spice up this simple table with stencils and paint, choosing numbers or sayings that are meaningful to your family. Store a pretty basket with throws on the bottom shelf for easy reach.

You Will Need:

» Miter saw
» Kreg Jig
» (5) 2" × 4" × 8' boards
» Clamps
» (60) 2½" Kreg Jig pocket hole screws
» Speed square
» Sander
» Medium sandpaper (150–220 grit)
» Fine sandpaper (320 grit)
» Minwax stain in Early American
» Staining pad

Cut List:

» (10) 22-inch 2" × 4"s (A)
» (10) 25-inch 2" × 4"s (B)

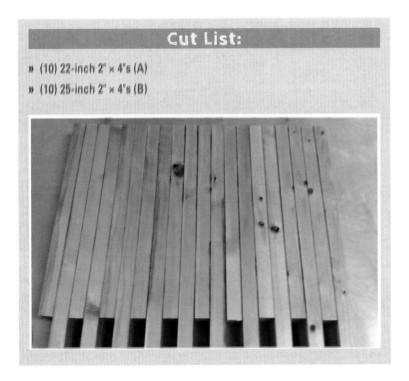

Staggered
Pocket Holes

1. Cut boards in the Cut List to size with the miter saw, or have them cut at your local home improvement store.

2. Using the Kreg Jig, drill two pocket holes on each end on the bottom of all ten (A) 2" × 4"s. There will be four holes total for each 2" × 4", and they should all be on the same side.

3. Now drill an additional 1 or 2 pocket holes in each board (A), staggering them. When all boards are together, holes will be staggered in the middle and not in a row.

4. Lay one 2" × 4" (A) with pocket holes facing up on your worktable. Clamp two 2" × 4"s (B) onto each end of (A) board, perpendicular to the table surface and the (A) board, making a U-shape. Attach using four Kreg Jig pocket hole screws.

5. Lay the frame on its side. Attach another (A) board 3" up from the U-opening. This is the first board of the shelf base of the table. Attach with Kreg Jig pocket hole screws. Be sure both of the (A) boards have pocket holes facing the same direction (down). Set the speed square to 3" so that each board is level and even.

STYLE FILE

Vary your board placement based on looks. You can place a heavier grained board beside a cleaner one, for example, to give your table personality and interest.

6. Repeat Steps 2 and 3 with (B) boards five more times to create five individual leg pieces.

7. Clamp all five leg pieces together, creating a box. Attach leg pieces together at the staggered pocket holes with Kreg Jig pocket hole screws.

8. Flip the table over and sand with a medium-grit sandpaper. Finish with fine sandpaper until smooth. If your table is a little uneven, put felt with tacky backing on the table leg bottoms to make it level.

9. Rub a thin coat of stain on, and wipe away excess after ten minutes. If you'd like, stencil on letters or numbers once the stain dries.

Crate Storage

This crate project is so simple, but it's highly sturdy and functional. This works well if you need more bookshelf storage, but the cool thing about this crate plan? You can stack two together to make a side table. You can store magazines or toys in the bottom crate and throws in the top. Functional and beautiful.

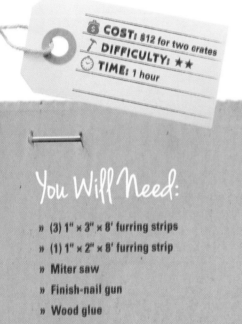

COST: $12 for two crates
DIFFICULTY: ★★
TIME: 1 hour

You Will Need:

» (3) 1" × 3" × 8' furring strips
» (1) 1" × 2" × 8' furring strip
» Miter saw
» Finish-nail gun
» Wood glue
» 1¼" finish nails
» Sander
» Stain or paint (optional)

Cut List:

» (11) 18-inch 1" × 3"s (A)
» (6) 12¼-inch 1" × 3"s (B)
» (4) 9½-inch 1" × 2"s (C)

1. Cut your boards to length with the miter saw, or have them cut at your local home improvement store.

2. Build the two bottom frames first. Attach two (B) boards to two (A) boards to make a rectangle. Clamp and nail into each end using 1¼" finish nails. Repeat to complete the frame.

3. Now build the top frame. Build the third frame exactly the same as the first two, but attach the long sides ⅝" above the short sides.

4. Attach five bottom (A) boards to one of the two frames using wood glue and 1¼" finish nails. The boards should be touching.

5. Now build the sides up. Attach the (C) boards to each of the four corners of the bottom frame, using several finish nails.

6. Slide the second frame on, but don't attach.

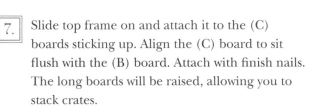

 7. Slide top frame on and attach it to the (C) boards sticking up. Align the (C) board to sit flush with the (B) board. Attach with finish nails. The long boards will be raised, allowing you to stack crates.

8. Center the middle frame, evenly spaced, and attach with finish nails.

9. Sand crates until smooth. If you'd like, stain or paint the crates. We used Rust-Oleum in Weathered Grey.

STYLE FILE

Personalize your crates by painting them in a bold color and stenciling a meaningful date on the side. If you're using your crates as storage, you can add hardware handles to the ends or a knob to the front. Dress these crates up in a multitude of ways!

STYLE FILE

Think about all the lights you can create with this method. You can cut a globe in half, hang a rattan ball, or turn virtually any basket or planter into a light fixture.

Basket Pendant Light

Lighting is so essential to the personality of a space. Think about it. When you move all the furniture out of your room, what is left? That's right: walls, a paint color, trim, and a light. Lighting sets the tone. This project is simple, inexpensive, and perfect for a more casual room. You start with any simple basket or container, drill a hole, and add a $15 light kit.

COST: $20
DIFFICULTY: ★★
TIME: 1 hour

You Will Need:

- » Apple basket
- » Craft paint
- » Small craft paintbrush
- » Drill with ⅜" drill bit
- » Pendant light kit
- » Small pulley
- » Natural colored rope

1. Start by painting the trim pieces around the basket to coordinate with your room. The light in the photos uses navy craft paint and was painted with a small craft paintbrush. Let dry.

2. Drill two holes into the bottom of the basket, one for the light kit cord and one for the rope used to hang the light.

3. Run the electrical cord from the kit through one of the holes.

4. Run the length of rope through the other hole and through the pulley (which is only decorative). Thread the rope through to create three loops so the cord is covered more.

5. Remove your current light fixture and hang your new basket pendant lamp. If you don't know how to reconnect electrical wires, hire a licensed electrician to replace the light for you.

Lantern Chandelier

You Will Need:

» Lantern/chandelier
» FrogTape
» Annie Sloan Chalk Paint in Coco
» Paintbrush
» Miss Mustard Seed's White Wax
(optional)

You know all of those brass chandeliers in your home, or the ones you see while perusing the flea market? With a little paint and tape, you can create a new light fixture that is all your own and looks virtually brand new.

1. Begin by cleaning and taping off your light fixture so no paint will get on the glass. Be sure to cover any cords or light bulb sockets as well.

2. Lightly brush one coat of Coco onto your lantern to create the appearance of aged brass or stone. Let dry.

3. To get the look pictured, you can rub some Miss Mustard Seed's White Wax over the paint for more of a washed finish. Feel free to let a little of the brass peek through.

4. While your lantern is drying, remove your old light fixture.

5. Replace your light fixture with the new chandelier. If you do not feel comfortable reattaching electrical wires, hire a licensed electrician to hang your fixture.

6. Add light bulbs, and let your new piece shine!

HANDY HOW-TO

Be very careful changing out your light fixtures. If in doubt, hire a licensed electrician to hang it for you.

245

Parting Words

No one told me that writing a blog could lead to inspiring people. Especially since I don't always feel inspirational; as a matter of fact, our life, in my eyes, is perfectly normal. I wanted to create this book for *you*, for someone with limited time and a limited budget, so that you could create in your everyday home; so that your "normal" might look a bit different.

It is my greatest hope that these projects and tips leave you inspired, and equip you with ideas and a spark to get started, to paint, to build, to craft; a spark to fully live where you are, embrace the imperfections, and create among them anyway.

As you create, may your home become your canvas, and your life the medium. May the projects you tackle be less about finishing, but more about how you feel creating them and living with them. May your home be completely *yours* from this point forward—perfectly imperfect, indeed.

Thanks

I am filled with gratitude as I write the last few words of this book. It seems fitting that I saved the thanking for the end, when I am tired and worn and words are blurring and have fed my children too many fast-food meals.

I am thankful still.

Thank you to the people at F+W Media, Inc. and Adams Media, who thought I might be able to pull this book off. Thank you to my editor, Maria Ribas, who believed in me, and made writing the book possible.

To my parents and my brother: Thank you for raising me to strive, to pursue, to hold my own. Thank you for your willingness to teach me at all times, never allowing me to settle at being less than my best. Thank you for supporting me all those years, and encouraging me now.

To my husband, Matt: This life would mean very little without you in it. I found you, that weird, silly person with whom I am meant to spend my days. Thank you for dealing with my extra workload, and for your ability to love and support me while always challenging me to be better. Thank you for being my person.

To my little ones, Grayson and Ava . . . oh, the places I hope to see you go. Thank you both for dealing with frozen waffles over the last few months, and for your help at the shop. Thank you for being such flexible little people, and for all the Grace you have given me. I love you more than you'll ever know, and am inspired to live purposefully for you.

I have to thank our team at Perfectly Imperfect, and for those that pitched in during this hectic season. To Natalie, Adam, Julie, Ryan, Lori, Amanda, Kaitlyn, Lindsay Bolton (at Chena Designs), Jason, and Regina Garay; thank you all for what you do to grow and further our brand, take care of our customers and readers, and make *Perfectly Imperfect* far more than a dot on the Web.

To my "in real life" blogging friends, Marian Parsons and Ashley Mills: Thank you both for always supporting me, praying with me, and understanding me. Thank you to Jenny and Lisa for being the kind of friends who loved me from the beginning. You are all amazing, and your encouragement during this process means the world. You girls are my heroes.

To the bloggers who contributed projects: we are honored and are in awe of your talent and creativity . . . thank you for sharing your work with us!

Thank you to Candace Nelson, for taking the loveliest photos of our family for this book.

Thank you to Julie and Sara for help with projects, and Kaitlyn, who did the photo editing for this book. I literally could not have finished the book on time without you, sweet girls.

To my readers, I must say that you all have been the surprise of my life. You came out of nowhere, sweep me off my feet and take me soaring. You inspire me, and I want to try, in my own way, to inspire you. I am beyond grateful to have you in our lives.

Last, but certainly not least, I thank my God for restoring me, for giving me Grace on the days I need it most, and the days I forget to ask. For accepting me as I am: imperfect.

Standard U.S./Metric Measurement Conversions

VOLUME CONVERSIONS

U.S. Volume Measure	Metric Equivalent
⅛ teaspoon	0.5 milliliter
¼ teaspoon	1 milliliter
½ teaspoon	2 milliliters
1 teaspoon	5 milliliters
½ tablespoon	7 milliliters
1 tablespoon (3 teaspoons)	15 milliliters
2 tablespoons (1 fluid ounce)	30 milliliters
¼ cup (4 tablespoons)	60 milliliters
⅓ cup	90 milliliters
½ cup (4 fluid ounces)	125 milliliters
⅔ cup	160 milliliters
¾ cup (6 fluid ounces)	180 milliliters
1 cup (16 tablespoons)	250 milliliters
1 pint (2 cups)	500 milliliters
1 quart (4 cups)	1 liter (about)
1 gallon	3.8 liters

WEIGHT CONVERSIONS

U.S. Weight Measure	Metric Equivalent
½ ounce	15 grams
1 ounce	30 grams
2 ounces	60 grams
3 ounces	85 grams
¼ pound (4 ounces)	115 grams
½ pound (8 ounces)	225 grams
¾ pound (12 ounces)	340 grams
1 pound (16 ounces)	454 grams

LENGTH

U.S.	Metric
1 inch	2.54 cm
1 foot	30.48 cm

Index

Note: Page numbers in *italics* indicate projects.

About the Author

Shaunna West began her journey of creating beauty in her home (on a budget) in 2009. Along with her husband, Matt, and two kids, Grayson and Ava, whom they homeschool, she tackled one room at a time, completely transforming the look and feel of their home without breaking the bank. Her website, *Perfectly Imperfect*, quickly grew from a hobby to a business within the first year, landing her work in home decor magazines like *Cottages & Bungalows, Country Living,* and *Flea Market Style*, on websites like *Design Sponge*, Pottery Barn Kids, and *Apartment Therapy*, and on television on *The Nate Berkus Show*.

She and her family live in Alabama where they write their blog and run their retail and online shops, *www.perfectlyimperfectshop.com*. On her blog, she shares daily inspiration and real ideas on how to celebrate the imperfection in your homes, the day to day of a creative entrepreneur and business owner, furniture makeovers, room reveals, and the simple projects that make her house a home.

There are many new exciting ventures on the horizon for the team at Perfectly Imperfect. For daily inspiration from a real life imperfect mama/entrepreneur and her family, visit their website at *www.perfectlyimperfectblog.com*.